HORIZON

MARCH, 1961 · VOLUME III, NUMBER 4

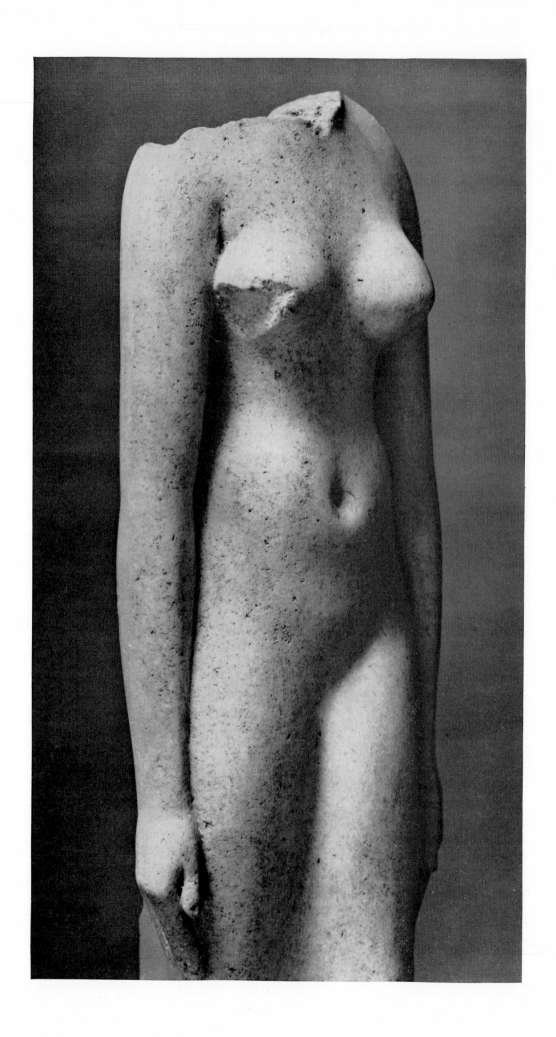

HORIZON

A Magazine of the Arts

MARCH, 1961 · VOLUME III, NUMBER 4

PUBLISHER
James Parton

EDITOR
Joseph J. Thorndike, Jr.
MANAGING EDITOR
William Harlan Hale
ASSOCIATE EDITORS
Ralph Backlund
Robert Emmett Ginna
ASSISTANT EDITORS
Ada Pesin
Jane Wilson
CONTRIBUTING EDITOR
Margery Darrell

EDITORIAL ASSISTANTS
Shirley Abbott, Caroline Backlund,
Wendy Buehr, Alan Doré

COPY EDITOR
Mary Ann Pfeiffer
Assistants: Rita Resnikoff, Ruth H. Wolfe

ART DIRECTOR
Irwin Glusker
Associate Art Director: Elton Robinson

ADVISORY BOARD
Gilbert Highet, *Chairman*
Frederick Burkhardt   Oliver Jensen
Marshall B. Davidson   Jotham Johnson
Richard M. Ketchum   John Walker

EUROPEAN CONSULTING EDITOR
J. H. Plumb
Christ's College, Cambridge

EUROPEAN BUREAU
Gertrudis Feliu, *Chief*
28 Quai du Louvre, Paris

CIRCULATION DIRECTOR
Richard V. Benson

HORIZON is published every two months by
American Horizon, Inc., a subsidiary of American
Heritage Publishing Co., Inc., 551 Fifth Avenue,
New York 17, N. Y.
Single Copies: $3.95
Annual Subscriptions: $18.00 in the U.S. & Can.
$19.00 elsewhere

Title registered U.S. Patent Office.
Second-class postage paid at New York, N.Y.

HORIZON welcomes contributions but can assume
no responsibility for such unsolicited material.

THE LOTUS AND THE ROBOT | *by Arthur Koestler* | 4

NEW YORK'S NEW WAVE OF MOVIE MAKERS
by Elizabeth Sutherland | 12

IN SEARCH OF PARADISE | *by Santha Rama Rau* | 20

CORBUSIER'S CLOISTER | *by Cranston Jones* | 34

THE THEATER OF FORM AND ANTI-FORM | *by Walter Kerr* | 42

THE KNIGHTS OF THE MALTESE CROSS | *by Edith Simon* | 48

ON STAGE: LEONTYNE PRICE | *by Richard Murphy* | 72

ON STAGE: GOLD AND FIZDALE | *by Jay S. Harrison* | 74

POUSSIN | *by Pierre Schneider* | 76

BOOKS: THE BIBLE IS GIVEN NEW SPEECH | *by Gilbert Highet* | 94

MOVIES: NEO-REALISMO REVISITED | *by Jean Stafford* | 98

ADVERTISING: TODAY'S TEMPLE OF TALENT | *by Stephen White* | 101

THEATER: HUMAN BEINGS AND SUBSTITUTES | *by Robert Hatch* | 102

GARGOYLES FOR THE MACHINE AGE | *by John Canaday* | 104

VOLTAIRE: "HE TAUGHT US TO BE FREE" | *by Harold Nicolson* | 114

YOUR FRIENDLY FIDVCIARY | *by Oliver Jensen* | 120

FRASCONI'S BRIO WITH A BOOK | | 122

COVER: Embodying the exotic grace of one of the few surviving island paradises of our time, a Balinese dancing girl appears in her ceremonial headdress, or *galungan*, before the camera of a visiting American, Ewing Krainin. She is costumed for the *legong*, a religious pantomime accompanied by classical Balinese music and narration. Her *galungan* is a jewel-studded crown made of leather dipped in gold and surmounted by *semodja* flowers sacred to the Hindu religion. Trained in the dance since early childhood and chosen for her beauty, she is no more than twelve. An article by Santha Rama Rau on Bali and other still unruined retreats around the globe begins on page 20.

FRONTISPIECE: This small limestone torso of a girl, or goddess, is, surprisingly, not Greek but Egyptian. It was carved probably in the years from 300 to 275 B.C., toward the end of the long history of Egyptian art, when the Ptolemies of Macedonian-Greek origin came to rule over the Nile Kingdom. The interest of Egyptian sculptors of this period in the female form was due to Greek influence, but this votive statue is thoroughly Egyptian in its symmetry, tranquility, and posture, lacking the movement and emotion of contemporary Greek sculpture. Only twenty inches high, it is one of the many outstanding pieces brought together this winter by Bernard V. Bothmer at the Brooklyn Museum for the first comprehensive showing anywhere of Egyptian sculpture of the Late Period (700 B.C.–A.D. 100).

THE LOTUS AND THE ROBOT

Like a diver with the bends, Japan now suffers the agonies of its too swift exposure to the machine age

By ARTHUR KOESTLER

As many Westerners have done before him, Arthur Koestler recently set out to discover whether the presumably more spiritual East had "any answer to offer to our perplexities and deadlocked problems." His conclusions will appear in a new book, The Lotus and the Robot, *to be published this spring by Macmillan. Here are his observations on Japan, a country that in his view has not yet resolved the differences between its own exquisitely nuanced culture and the bolder patterns it has imported from the West—for example, the contrast between the courtesy of the Japanese at home and their boorish behavior on public transport (above). That, he learned, is because trains are* modan—*modern—and tradition provides no precedent or guidance in the situation.*

During my stay in Japan I went through three emotional phases. The first few days I lived in a colorful haze of euphoria. This was followed by a period of mounting exasperation, occasionally verging on hatred. In the third phase some bits of the puzzle began to fall into their places with a succession of almost audible clicks, and progress in understanding led to the acceptance of what Zen-inclined Japanese call "the such-ness of things." The three phases were not neatly separated in time; towards the end of my stay they would alternate in quick succession within a single day or hour—a rather unsettling experience. Life in Japan may be compared to a scented bath which gives you electric shocks at unexpected moments. That metaphor is as good as any.

圖之道鐵繩高

Japanese tend to think of railways as "new," even though their first was opened in 1872—shortly before this drawing was made

The first phase of sensuous and sensual delight is the tourist's inevitable reaction to a culture with a surface polish of utterly refined pretty-prettiness, smiling ceremonial, kneeling waitresses, paper-screen houses, dolls, kimonos, and above all, an atmosphere with an erotic flicker like the crisp sparks from a comb drawn through a woman's hair—a guilt-free eroticism which Europe has not known since antiquity. I responded to all this the more readily as, coming from India, I felt as if I were suddenly emerging in my bathyscaph from the pressure of the black deep, with its tangles of ghostly seaweed and primeval monsters, into a brilliant, sun-lit world. In India I had almost forgotten that you could walk on a pavement without fear of stepping on a huddled

figure, that cafés, bars, and theaters existed; accustomed to the sight of females swaddled in shapeless cotton sheets, I was thrilled to rediscover that women have curves—not to mention their disconcerting habit of glancing straight, if slantingly, into your eyes, from iris to iris, instead of pretending to be struck blind, deaf, and dumb by the shameful secret of the Lord's Creation. In a word, it was a relief to live through Saint Augustine's *Confessions* in reverse gear, as it were.

Strolling through the Ginza in the spring sunshine was like being taken to a toyshop in one's childhood: huge, gaudy balloons, hung with streamers, were floating in the sky; helicopters were humming like dragonflies; uniformed chauffeurs

5

A new Japanese addiction is tranquilizers, sold everywhere without prescription and here proffered by a cutout in a drugstore doorway.

were dancing around their parked shiny cars with feather-dusters, like chambermaids in the first scene of a French comedy; girl guides, waving yellow flags, were leading an Indian file of cow-eyed rustics through the roaring traffic of their capital; two elderly gentlemen in black morning coats were bowing and bowing and bowing each other through the revolving doors of a bank; earnest infants with running noses, strapped to their mothers' backs, were riding through the world as if in kangaroo pouches put on the wrong side; everybody seemed to be taking snapshots of everybody else, and buying little bunches of scented violets from dignified urchins, and giggling at their narrow escapes from kamikaze taxi drivers with music streaming from their transistor radios.

Later on, during the rush hour, when the whole town seems to thrash out in a kind of frenzied fit, charging into the electric trains with no holds barred, smiles effaced and courtesies suspended, the shy young men are transformed into vicious brutes, and the frail Misses Butterfly into all-in wrestlers. Then the lights go up, the town changes into a bubble bath of colored neon, and the bars, restaurants, and geisha houses provide pleasures for all incomes and tastes, enjoyed with equal decorum and in the same spirit of innocence.

This phase lasted for about a week. With some visitors it lasts throughout their whole stay, and half the literature on Japan, from Lafcadio Hearn to contemporary travelogues, reflects the euphoric stage, with Kabuki, Nō, Zen, tea ceremony, and flower arrangement brought in under the same romantic angle. The majority of Westerners who become involved with the country one way or another tend to become

either Japan-addicts or Japan-haters. The Japanese way of life contains a challenge to Western man which provokes extreme responses.

During the first phase one looks as if through the wrong end of the telescope at a distant and idealized scene, free from the blemishes of close involvement; and one feels envious of a spirit of graceful hedonism which the Westerner lost a long time ago. During the second phase other aspects of Japanese life come to the fore, and these are no longer seen through the lenses, but as reflections in a distorting mirror, caricatures of our Western civilization held uncomfortably close to one's face.

Many Japanese, for instance, walk through life wearing anesthetists' masks, which cover their mouth and nostrils. These masks, or pads, of cotton are worn by men and women of all ages in the streets, in buses and trains, in cinemas, schools, and at home. On the day of my arrival, when I saw the first muzzled couple walk past, I thought they were victims of leprosy or some other frightful disease. Then I learnt that the masks were meant as a protection against inhaling germs from the air and exhaling germs on others—a triumph of *modan*—modern—ideas of hygiene. I was irresistibly reminded of Gulliver's voyage to Laputa, where some people carried huge bundles on their backs, filled with models of all things they could think of, and conversed by pointing at the appropriate models because they held the effort of speaking to be unhealthy for the lungs.

If the masks are a harmless travesty of Western "scientific living," the nation-wide addiction to *tranki*—tranquilizers—can hardly be called that. It struck Japan with "typhoon force"—as *Time* magazine had it—in the autumn of 1956; three years later there were about fifty different brands on the market, all sold without prescription, praised on huge billboards by unscrupulous advertisers who invite their customers to take a couple of tablets three or four times a day, or even to "take as many as you want any time you have worries." Drugs with the opposite effect are used with equal readiness: the trainer of the Olympic team of swimmers admitted in 1958 in a statement to the press that his athletes had been pumped full of vitamin injections before the Japan-U.S.A. swimming contest, and that they intended to continue this practice on similar occasions.

An even more depressing aspect of "scientific living" is reflected in the Japanese ways of family planning. The Japanese have succeeded in halving their birth rate—but at the price of one and a half million abortions per year. A law, passed a few years ago, makes abortions legal for a fee of about three dollars if the expectant mother can prove economic hardship or impairment of health—which is a pure formality. Contraceptives are also legal but unpopular, except among the upper classes and in extramarital relations; the result is the slaughter of the unborn with its concomitant ill effects on the women.

Another major curse of a different kind is miniature electronics. Transistor radios have spread in Japan like myxomatosis, and though their effects are not as deadly, in the long run they must affect the nervous system of the millions who carry the insidious gadgets all day in their handbags or trouser pockets. Sometimes in a bus, when the announcer's voice seemed to pipe out from inside the body of my impassive neighbor, I took him for a ventriloquist. On a train journey from Fukuoka to Nagasaki, which takes about three and a half hours, three pocket-transistor sets were loudly and simultaneously transmitting three different programs from window ledges in the carriage. Nobody seemed to mind.

This train journey was part of a trip, in the company of English friends, to a popular hot-spring resort, which gave us an idea of the terrors of modern Japanese holidays. The Unzen Amakusa National Park on Kyushu, the southernmost island of Japan, is dominated by an extinct volcano; it is surrounded by the sea, has splendid scenery with steaming geysers and fumaroles, in addition to hot-water swimming pools for mixed nude bathing, archery grounds, tennis courts, bars, and pachinko parlors. The latter have rows of pin-tables, all of uniform type, standing in uniform lines, worked by addicts with grimly set jaws who, deafened by the monotonous burr-zurr of thousands of tiny metal balls, hypnotized by their incessant dancing and spinning, impersonate the damned in a Sartresque limbo.

At Obama, a seaside resort, we boarded a huge and shiny motorbus to the dead volcano, Mount Unzen. It was crowded with excursionists; the moment we started, a pretty hostess in a blue airline uniform appeared with a portable microphone to explain to us everything we saw. It took the bus about an hour and a half to climb the three thousand feet to Unzen, and during that time her soft patter, hoarsened by the loudspeaker, never let up for a minute. When in danger of drying up, she would point at a shop above the last hairpin bend and inform us that it used to be a millinery shop but now it was a confectionery shop. At this all the heads in the bus would turn in the indicated direction, and all eyes would assume that glazed stare which indicates the process of digesting information; for the Japanese believe in the nutritive value of information regardless of the subject—they ingest knowledge wholesale as a boa swallows a rabbit.

On the top of the mountain there was, as yet, no loudspeaker. But there were arrows directing us to "View Point No. 1" and on to No. 2 and No. 3. Each viewpoint consisted of a small wooden platform, and each platform in its turn was occupied by all members of the excursion simultaneously, blocking out each other's view. By walking first to View Point No. 3 and then anticlockwise to No. 1, we three foreigners had each platform to ourselves. But we could feel the Japanese blushing for us.

The best customers of *tranki* are the university students. On my second day in Tokyo, driving towards Yokohama, I saw a large, silent, anxious crowd in front of an imposing public edifice. I stopped the taxi, expecting to see a funeral cortège emerge from the building, and learnt that it was Tokyo University and that the mournful crowd consisted of the parents, brothers, and sisters of the candidates who, behind the barred gates, were undergoing the ordeal of the entrance examinations. I further learnt that there were 38,000 candidates for the 6,000 available vacancies, in other words, that over six out of seven candidates would fail. Among the 33,000 failures, over 13,000 will more or less seriously contemplate suicide—according to the statistics of a prominent Tokyo psychiatrist, Professor Takeyama; but only eighteen will actually kill themselves.

Since the new education law was passed in 1947 by the American occupation authorities, universities have been shooting up like mushrooms, the annual number of enrollments is approaching the one-million mark, and a university degree has become a *conditio sine qua non* for obtaining a clerical job. To a middle-class family the money spent on the candidate's education meant a considerable sacrifice. To the candidate himself it meant being burdened with a heavy *on*—an obligation that must be repaid under penalty of disgrace before the world and oneself.

All my remarks so far refer to elements in Japanese life which were either directly copied from the West or developed on imitative lines. These elements added together constitute one aspect of modern Japan. But is it a reflection of the West in a distorting mirror—or in a true mirror, which magnifies blemishes not otherwise noticed?

The mirror in ancient Japanese tradition was a symbol that meant almost the opposite of what it means to us. It was not an instrument of vanity, but of contemplation, and is often seen in Shinto shrines. The person gazing into the mirror does not do so to examine his appearance, but to gaze through the "door of the soul," his eyes reflected in the glass, into his innermost self. It is a method of short-circuiting his self-conscious, "observing self"; what he sees reflected in the glass is the original purity and calm of his spiritual being.

Western man, on the other hand, either gazes at himself in the looking glass in the attitude of Narcissus—or the shaving mirror turns into a picture of Dorian Gray. When we see ourselves reflected in the most Westernized nation in Asia, it is that ghastly experience that comes to the mind; the mirror reveals the image of a robot with built-in duodenal ulcers. Hence our violent reactions: the lotusland seen through the reversed telescope evokes our nostalgia for the golden age before the Fall; the robotland reflected in the mirror makes us shudder. This is, of course, an exaggerated reaction, for the reflection in the mirror is only half the truth about Japan, and half the truth about the West. But this is the only half common to both, and there's the rub.

However, the contrast between lotusland and robotland exists not only in the beholder's eye. The Japanese themselves have failed to reconcile the two planes of existence, and two half-truths together do not make an integrated whole. All nations are bundles of contradictions, but nowhere except in Japan are the conflicting strands so neatly sorted out and arranged on two mutually exclusive levels which alternate in taking control and produce dual personalities in a dual culture as sharply defined as a Japanese color print.

This unique quality of contemporary Japan derives from the uniqueness of Japanese history. When, after two hundred and fifty years of hermetic isolation and mental inbreeding, the Meiji Restoration of 1868 suddenly threw the islands open to the world, the results were as explosive as if the windows of a pressurized cabin had been broken. Nothing similar had in fact happened to any race in recorded history. Within a single generation the pent-up energies of the nation exploded in a frantic effort to catch up with everything that the West had accomplished in half a millennium. They succeeded to a spectacular degree; at the beginning of the twentieth century Japan had become one of the leading military and industrial powers of the world.

By the force of circumstances this result could only be achieved through learning-by-imitation. The Industrial Revolution of the eighteenth and nineteenth centuries in the West had grown organically out of the Scientific Revolution of the seventeenth century, whose roots reach back to the revival of Greek learning between the twelfth and sixteenth centuries. The Japanese could not be expected to duplicate the whole process, to produce their own Roger Bacons, Isaac Newtons, and James Watts. They had to proceed in reverse; starting with the mechanical copying of the end products of the applied sciences, they had to work their way back to the theoretical foundations—from Edison to Galileo.

The starting point of this evolution in reverse gear is a bronze howitzer which Commodore Perry, after forcing his entry into Tokyo Bay, had presented as a gift to the Japanese authorities. A year or two later they fired a salute to the American fleet from a battery of "handsome bronze howitzers, exactly copied in every respect from the one Commodore Perry gave them; every appointment about the gun, down to the smallest particular, was exactly copied: percussion locks, drag ropes, powder or cartridge holder and all." They had to begin by copying mechanically, since they were not yet able to understand the exact purpose of the various parts of the gun; their eagerness to copy was not due to any inherent imitative tendency in the Japanese character, but to the hunger for knowledge of a people just emerging from two hundred and fifty years of solitary confinement.

Western science and technology acted as a Trojan Horse; out of its belly poured alien philosophies, fashions, political concepts, attitudes to life. They could not be copied like Perry's bronze howitzers, and they did not blend with the traditional culture.

A Japanese who lived for four score years, from 1865 to 1945, would have witnessed developments which in European history occupy several centuries: Absolute Monarchy, Constitutional Monarchy, Liberalism, Imperialist Expansion, Military Dictatorship, Totalitarian Fascism, Foreign Occupation. He would also have witnessed the disestablishment of Buddhism, the proclamation of Shinto as the State Religion, and the subsequent disestablishment of Shinto—changes which struck at the very root of ethical beliefs. Furthermore, he would have watched a remarkable transformation in the physique of his younger compatriots, from the average height of five feet one inch of conscripts at the turn of the century to five feet four inches in 1952—an increase of three inches in fifty years.

As if to dramatize these developments Nature contributed tremors and flames. There were disastrous earthquakes in 1892 and 1894; the Imperial Palace burnt down in 1873; most of the capital was destroyed by the Great Earthquake and Fire of 1923, which claimed 150,000 victims. The 700,000 houses which had gone up in flames were rebuilt in a hurry—and destroyed again twenty years later, in 1945. That was the year in which the two man-made suns descended on Hiroshima and Nagasaki—but the two conventional fire raids on Tokyo, earlier in the same year, had claimed another 100,000 victims and reduced the capital to charred rubble for the second time within a generation.

In the course of the next five years the first conquering invader whom the Japanese had known in history imposed a revolution which transformed the nation even more radically than the Meiji reform. That had come from within; the new regime was enforced by the Occupation Authority. The State religion was abolished, the school textbooks of history and geography were burnt, the Prime Minister was hanged. The Emperor was no longer a god, the Army and Navy no longer existed. Forty per cent of the total area under cultivation was confiscated from the absentee landlords and distributed among the tenants; a new constitution established Western-style Parliamentary rule; women were given the vote and legal status equal to men; compulsory education was extended to nine years, and the number of universities mushroomed from forty-odd to nearly five hundred.

Japan absorbed Western science and technology like a sponge; but Western culture and the Western way of life were skin grafts from an alien donor which, though eagerly accepted, never took.

With its population of nine million citizens, Tokyo-Yokohama is, according to Japanese statistics, the largest city in the world; yet its streets have no names and the houses have no serial numbers. During the Occupation the Americans tried to introduce some rudimentary order into that colossal labyrinth by naming the most important thoroughfares A Avenue to Z Avenue, and 1st Street to 60th Street. But when the Occupation ended, the municipal authorities refused to renew even the few decaying street signs which the Americans had put up at the main junctions; and no Japanese will ever refer to N Avenue or X Street. He will name the district and subdistrict in which he lives and then draw an artistic map. The more important shops, restaurants, hospitals, offices, have cards with printed maps; and the maps, as often as not, are found to be either incomplete or misleading.

When I questioned Japanese acquaintances on the subject, the usual answer was: "The streets in your towns are laid out in geometrical order, but ours are winding and tortuous, so it would be impossible to number them." When informed that the streets of Paris and London were equally crooked, he would express his delighted surprise and change the subject. He would, for instance, point out that Tokyo Tower is twenty feet higher than the Eiffel Tower and would perhaps add with a chuckle that this fact was never mentioned during the recent visit of the French Trade Delegation, lest they should lose face.

Other answers were more direct: "Street names are all right for Westerners, but we find our way without them." The truth is, they do not. Among the anonymous millions who inhabit the capital the large majority lead a life which is confined to their immediate neighborhood; they shop along their street and have few friends or outside contacts, whose houses they locate by memory. The higher strata of the population attach private maps to invitations or business appointments, or send their cars. Postmen must know their clients in the district by name or locate the addresses by house-to-house inquiry. Taxi drivers follow a similar procedure; the extra time one must usually allow them for finding an address is about half an hour. The same applies to ambulances and the fire brigade, when they are called in an emergency.

An American editor has described his incredulous astonishment when he visited the building of one of Japan's mammoth daily newspapers with a circulation of four to five million. He saw its scientific wonders, from the rotation presses in the basement, through the telephotographic and speed-graphic equipment, to the helicopter park and the carrier pigeons on the roof; he saw every trick and gadget of mass communication, except—typewriters. To our minds a journalist without a typewriter is like a samurai without a sword; in Japan not only newspaper offices but business offices and government departments must do without them. Fantastic as it seems, business in one of the great commercial empires of our time is almost universally transacted by handwriting—and without keeping carbons for the record.

The reason is that a Japanese typewriter must have 2,000 to 3,000 keys to provide even the limited vocabulary of the popular press; for higher literary purposes it would have to possess 3,000 to 4,000 signs (although I have been told that a revolutionary kind of typewriter using a mere nine hundred keys will shortly appear on the market). That is the number of Chinese ideograms which the average educated Japanese is supposed to be able to read and write correctly; and each of these is an abstract design in miniature, requiring up to twenty-five strokes of the brush or pen. As if this were not enough, the Japanese script has been further complicated by past attempts to simplify it. The Chinese ideograms were introduced in the early centuries of our era; be-

In the Westernized surroundings of the Ginza one still sees men "bowing and bowing and bowing" to each other in the traditional way.

fore that the Japanese had no written language. From the eighth century onward a movement developed to use ideograms, drawn in a simplified form, for denoting sounds instead of ideas. Thus a phonetic script developed, whose signs, however, expressed not single letters but syllables; it was not quite a phonetic alphabet, but a syllabary; and instead of one system, there were two. One is called *kata-kana*, the other *hira-gana*; each has fifty signs. This was still a far cry from the simplicity of, say, the Hebrew or Greek alphabets with their twenty-odd signs; but it was nevertheless a great step forward and led to the first flowering of Japanese literature in the eleventh and twelfth centuries. Its pioneers, oddly enough, were the ladies at the Emperor's Court; they were sophisticated and bored, and took to writing languid diaries in the phonetic script. The great classic novel of Japan, *The Tale of Genji,* dates from that period; its author was the Lady Murasaki. One wonders what would have happened to Japanese literature if it had been left to the use of the phonetic script—and preferably to the women, who, burdened by fewer social responsibilities than the men, preserved throughout the ages a more spontaneous approach to life. That was perhaps the reason why the *sensei,* the learned, pedantic scholars who are the bane of Japanese culture, would not acquiesce in a phonetic script that made writing an altogether too simple and spontaneous affair. They persisted in writing in Chinese—the equivalent of the medieval Latin used by European scholars—whereas the ladies wrote in Japanese, using *kana*; and when, in the end, the national language carried the day, the scholars still stuck to the Chinese ideograms. Thus arose, in the course of the centuries, the Sino-Japanese hybrid script, which survives to this day and is the most cumbersome written language in existence. It is a combination of Chinese ideograms, which denote concepts, and various forms of *kana*, which denote sounds. To complicate matters a little further, *kana* is not only used to fill in the grammatical gaps between the uninflected ideograms, but also as a kind of parallel comment, to indicate the pronunciation or to clarify the meaning of the former. This is necessary because many Chinese ideograms have several different meanings in Japanese; and vice versa, the mere sound of a Japanese word rendered in phonetic *kana* may mean a dozen and more different things. The result is a script which combines, as it were, Egyptian hieroglyphics with Pitman's shorthand signs and musical notations for several instruments. If one glances at a printed page, the Chinese ideograms stick out like massive scars among the graceful crow's-feet of *kana* and *hira-gana*—the result of another, much earlier, cultural skin graft.

That is why the Japanese have transistor radios but have to do without typewriters. Only the big banks and business trusts possess huge machines which are a luxury, like electronic computers. The typical modern Japanese business firm, with its high-pressure sales methods, transacting its business through a host of calligraphers, is once again Gulliver in Laputa.

A reform of the written language would not only do away with a major hindrance which clogs the wheels of the nation's affairs; it would also save years of heavy intellectual grind

Japanese bars, night clubs, and geisha houses "provide pleasures for all incomes and tastes"—and often, as below, unabashedly advertise them.

MARC RIBOUD—MAGNUM

in the life of every successive generation. It would have even more far-reaching consequences, because the confusions and ambiguities of the Japanese script are reflected in the structure of Japanese thinking. And that, perhaps, is the cause of their instinctive resistance against reform of the script. They refuse to part with the comforts of ambiguity and prefer the printed page, like the streets of the capital, to remain a labyrinth where only the initiate, guided by his intuition, can find his way—or lose it in agreeable detours.

I remarked to an elderly professor about the contrast between the courtesy of the Japanese at home and the brutality of their behavior on public transport. "But is that not natural?" he answered in a tone of surprise. "Railways are new."

The first railway, between Tokyo and Yokohama, was opened in 1872, but railways are "new" in the sense in which everything that came since the opening of the country is "new." It means that tradition provides no precedent and no guidance for the proper way of behavior in the situation in question. Trains and buses exist, but they exist outside the traditional pattern, in a cultural no man's land where no rules of etiquette apply.

Similarly, electric lighting, European clothes, and Western water closets are situated in an aesthetic no man's land. In the austere surroundings of square boxes with sliding paper panels which make a Japanese house, every object, down to the smallest, is chosen with meticulous care, as if it were to be part of a museum—except for the naked electric bulb hanging from the ceiling, or the Woolworth standard lamp. They are useful but not part of the landscape, and aesthetic considerations such as are given to a sake cup or a flower vase do not apply to them; nor to European-style clothes and shoes, still regarded by the majority as civilian uniforms for office wear, which offer no scope for the expression of one's taste and personality—in contrast to Japanese clothes, into which they like to change as soon as they get home. The classic footwear are slippers in the house and *geta*—wooden clogs—outdoors; and the traditional Japanese housewife's attitude to European footgear is best described in that hilarious classic *The Honourable Picnic*. The lady is talking about her husband's shoes, which he has to wear at his office:

They are so inconvenient to take care of. A year or two ago I put them to wash with the *geta* in a basin of warm water. They sank to the bottom and the water soaked them through all the better. But then, impossible to get them dry. In vain I put them on the very embers in the stove, they scorched and smelled and that was all. And by reason of going out with wet shoes, my husband caught bronchitis. It even seems that they shrank and gave him pain, as well. So this winter, in spite of the bad weather we had, I prohibited the maid to touch them, and in spring they had the mud on them still of New Year's. It was very ugly to see.

That lady was evidently a member of Japan's psychological *maquis*, the unconscious resisters, the smiling saboteurs of Western-style clothes, road signs, plumbing, manners, customs, and languages. On the plumbing front the *maquis* operates with particular success. The interior of the house is kept scrupulously clean, as it always has been—except for the W. C., which is a post-Meiji import. It is either permanently blocked or installed without the odor-insulating siphon; while outside the house the open sewer runs, as often as not, along the front wall, with a plank serving as a bridge to the entrance. The Japanese have a most delicate sense of scent, but they become smell-blind when it suits them.

The least successful grafts were those in art and philosophy. They imported, together with machine tools and railway engines, German metaphysics, French skepticism, and Russian nihilism; a Bismarckian form of government, with the French system of prefectures; Darwin and Beethoven, Chekhov and Rodin, K. Marx and H. Spencer, with polite impartiality; but somehow these component parts proved more difficult to assemble than cameras and motorcars. At Waseda University in Tokyo they built a faithful replica of a Shakespearean theater, which houses a Kabuki Museum; and one professor is reported to have spent his life in writing footnotes to *Beowulf* without knowing modern English.

On the printed sheet for the Tokyo University entrance examination, the first "correct answer" in the translation test was given as follows: "She should have told it to him when she found his failure." It was not a misprint, but a fair sample of how English is taught at Japanese universities. The first invitation I received from a Professor of English at one of the leading colleges began with: "Sir, I esteem it a high honour to write you this letter"; it ended with: "Of course, I have no intention of interfering in your private concerns or matters, or hurting you, except full of good-will. From the bottom of my heart I hope your good health." When we met, the Professor turned out to be a delightful person, who never realized how deeply involved he was with the *maquis*.

Japan is the most Westernized among the great Asiatic nations, with the highest standard of literacy and living, the highest achievements in the sciences and arts—yet the most drastically cut off from verbal commerce with the West. Even the surprisingly small number of Japanese intellectuals who profess to have studied English twist and torture the language out of all recognition.

It would be absurd to assume that the Japanese suffer from some inherent racial handicap which makes them unable to master a foreign language. If, in spite of their imitative genius, they are such awkard linguists, the explanation must rather be sought in certain idiosyncrasies rooted in the collective psyche—a term that sounds less abstract in Japan than elsewhere. Isolation both in the historical and geographical sense may be one factor; the absence of a phonetic alphabet, another—a language whose elements are not single sounds but syllables moves, as it were, in fixed phonetic grooves. But the main reason is perhaps the same unconscious resistance which makes them cling to their cumbersome and anachronistic script. They could no doubt master

the vocabulary, syntax, and grammar of a Western language —if they were willing to adopt the matter-of-fact type of thinking and the logical categories which the structure of that language implies. But this, it seems, is what they are unwilling or unable to do. To ask a Japanese to *think* in English terms amounts to asking an impressionistic landscape painter to adopt the methods of a land surveyor.

Though the graft never took, it prevented the growth of natural tissue. Tradition survived—stubbornly rather than triumphantly—but it ceased to develop. The Meiji era was one of rapid material progress and spiritual stagnation. The evolution of poetry and drama, of painting and music, architecture and interior decoration, came by and large to a standstill. Haiku and Nō, flower arrangement and tea ceremony, became more and more self-conscious rituals—fossil pleasures embedded in petrified aestheticism.

To the young they have little to offer. The *mobo* and *apureguru*—modern boy and *après-guerre* girl—live in a spiritual desert more scorching than that of their coevals in the West. They call themselves neither angry nor beat, but "the generation which lost its identity." For the simple-minded there is the pachinko parlor, American flicks, and *sutorippu*—striptease. For the highbrow, the dark cafeterias, beatnik affectations, and existential *Angst*. They admire T. S. Eliot, not because they read him, but because "The Waste Land" has become their slogan; and with an unerring instinct they extract from Western art and philosophy only those elements which nourish the traditional Japanese melancholia and self-pity, their feeling of "the Ah-ness of things." They are like an imaginary species of bees which, mutated by irradiation, are only attracted by bitter flowers, yielding a bitter honey.

They hate the robotland in which they live, and they hate themselves for succumbing to its temptations. They yearn for a lotusland which they know to have become an anachronism; yet they are unable to struggle free from its ancestral grip. At middle age, the majority revert, as previous generations did, to the ancient pattern—the frigid joys of moon-viewing in the abstract rock garden, and the stilted repartees of an equally middle-aged geisha concubine. But in each generation there was also a small minority searching for a new way of reconciling the two patterns. One day, no doubt, they will succeed; but that day is not yet.

The opening up of the country after a quarter-millennium of segregation made the nation resemble a diver suddenly breaking surface. The brutal change of pressure causes bubbles to form in his veins, and he suffers the agony known as the bends. In contrast to the small elite of Westernized leaders in India, who seem to me to be travelers in a bathyscaph isolated from their surroundings, the Japanese are a nation of skin divers. Unfortunately, they cannot go back into the pressure chamber to dissolve the bubbles by getting gradually de-pressurized. They must find some original cure for a malaise without precedent.

FRANCIS THOMPSON, one of America's most imaginative film makers, is best known for his N.Y., N.Y., completed in 1958. In it, by using special mirrors and lenses of his own design, he creates such engaging and witty semiabstract images of Manhattan as the distorted "floating" skyscrapers and automobile shown above. As a boy Thompson made his first movie by drawing successive pictures on a roll of adding-machine paper and pulling it through a shoe box with a peephole for a viewer. Always developing new methods, he has employed in his latest film, a documentary for the Atomic Energy Commission, a novel three-screen, triple-image technique. Thompson, a former painter, has always been susceptible to mechanical magnificence, and a sense of the beauty of technology permeates his work.

MAKERS

American movies and the men who make them have long been derided by European intellectuals as wedded to hackneyed characters and situations in pursuit of the dollar. But in the last few years these same foreign devotees of the cinema have welcomed a new force in movie making, emanating from New York—where fifty years ago the fresh art of the movies had its headquarters.

Ironically, while the films of the new school of New York have been winning acclaim from critics and audiences in Europe and harvesting prizes at international festivals there, they remain little known in the United States itself. For the fact is that although 600-odd movie theaters of the type called "art houses" dot the nation, most of them are devoted to no more artful exhibits than the *poitrine* of Mlle Bardot.

Several names have been given to the movement—"New American Cinema," "Spontaneous Cinema," and "American New Wave"—the last in deference to the current French film ferment (see the article "The New Wave," HORIZON, May, 1960). If it is a wave, it is still somewhat submerged so far as the American movie-goer is concerned. Moreover, some of its practitioners deny that it should even be termed a movement, since it is marked by such diversity among themselves. Its common denominator had best be expressed first in terms of what it is not. It is not Hollywood. It is a departure from the canon of full-length features built from a script of fiction and produced with professional casts under the controlled conditions of a sound stage. Its originators prefer the documentary and unusual; the subjects that interest them are ones that reflect contemporary life—sometimes in the raw. They explore these with a minimum of script and a maximum of improvisation, using nonprofessional or unknown actors, and relying upon actual locations and naturally available light wherever possible.

The boundaries of such approaches are broad. The work of eight principals of the New York group of film makers, which HORIZON samples here, ranges from a semi-abstract poem hymning the forms, colors, and motions of a great metropolis (Francis

TEXT CONTINUED ON PAGE 19

SIDNEY MEYERS, long a respected film editor and maker of documentaries, is an individualist whose talents are trenchantly displayed in The Savage Eye. *This indeed savage 67-minute study looks in Hogarthian terms at the seamy side of life in contemporary Los Angeles—any large city would have done as well, says Meyers—and follows a divorcee as she tries to recover from her broken marriage in a world of wrestling-match and strip-tease addicts, transvestites, and sufferers who line up for the ministrations of wholesale faith healers (above). Such scenes, caught from real life by half a dozen photographers, were put together with sequences involving actors by Meyers, producer Joseph Strick, and writer Ben Maddow during four years of weekend work. Meyers, who is also a painter, musician, and the holder of a Master's degree in Elizabethan literature, grew up on the Harlem streets that are the setting for* The Quiet One, *the tender story of a disturbed Negro child, which he directed and which won him international acclaim.*

ROBERT FRANK's reputation as graphic spokesman of the Beat Generation has been earned largely by his first film, Pull My Daisy. *Made in a Bowery loft in 1959, it chronicles a day of talk and antics by the poets Allen Ginsberg (above, supine) and Gregory Corso (seated), who are also joined by poet Peter Orlovsky, composer David Amram, and the painter Larry Rivers (appearing in the guise of a railroad brakeman). A narration as lyrical and lively as Frank's camerawork was provided by Jack Kerouac, who also wrote an introduction to* The Americans, *a book of candid and sardonic photographs taken by Frank during a two-year journey across America on a Guggenheim grant. A native of Switzerland, Frank has completed a new film,* The Sin of Jesus, *which explores fantasy's role in religious belief.*

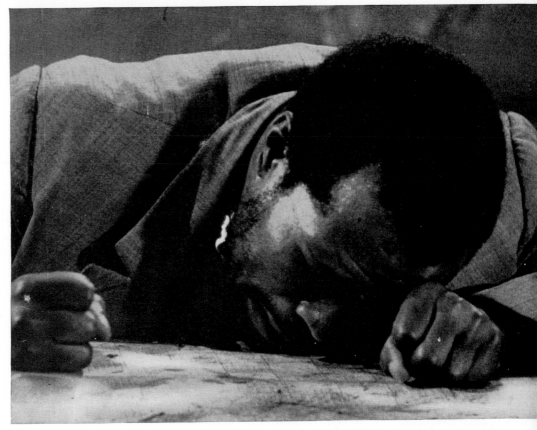

LIONEL ROGOSIN's motivation as a film maker is, he says, "to show what people try to avoid seeing." Driven by the conscience of the rich and by a temperamental sympathy for the underdog, Rogosin left the presidency of his family's textile business at 30 and, with a cameraman and a writer, went to live among the derelicts of New York's Skid Row, emerging in 1956 with an extraordinary documentary, On the Bowery. The next year Rogosin immersed himself in the Negro community of Johannesburg, South Africa; telling white officials there that he was simply filming a musical, he smuggled out of the country the footage of Come Back, Africa, a compassionate portrayal of Negro despair and rage (above) under apartheid. Now directing a documentary on peace movements, he says that his films "are made in the cutting room"; there he has had notable assistance from editor Carl Lerner.

JOHN CASSAVETES, a 31-year-old actor, gained sudden prominence among film makers in 1959 with Shadows, a feature-length study of race tensions and loneliness in Manhattan. The film's main characters are Negroes—a dark-skinned blues singer and his light-skinned brother and sister; its central incident, an affair between the sister and a white man; the last of its bruising episodes, a beating inflicted on the brother (above). Shadows grew out of improvisations in a drama workshop, and in directing it, Cassavetes allowed his actors to develop the rough story-line spontaneously. Despite extensive reshooting, the film cost only $40,000; its critical success here and abroad—the London Observer called it "convincing and original . . . a landmark"—has encouraged Cassavetes to make preparations for three new films, two of them to be set in Mexico.

SHIRLEY CLARKE is that rarity, a woman film director. For ten years a dancer, she brings to film making unusual gifts of rhythm, movement, and intensity, as well as a determination to take on man-sized subjects. Her documentary Skyscraper (1958) chronicled the rise of the 39-story Tishman Building at 666 Fifth Avenue with irony, beauty, and humor (above, a construction worker seen during a break). This winter the director—who turned to films in 1953—made her first full-length feature, The Connection, a screen version of the off-Broadway play about narcotic addicts by Jack Gelber. During its hectic month in production she made a comment that sums up the spirit in which she works: "This is such fun —like a marvelous game you want to win."

RICHARD LEACOCK *was only 14 when he made his first film—an account of the banana industry in the Canary Islands, then his home. The famous Robert Flaherty saw and remembered it and later used Leacock on the award-winning* Louisiana Story, *establishing him as one of the finest cameramen in the East. After photographing such short but noteworthy "pretty films" (his phrase for works that stress a beautiful image) as* Jazz Dance *and* Christopher and Me, *which he also directed, the London-born Leacock is again working on documentaries. Using highly portable synchronized sound and camera systems that achieve startling immediacy and directness, Leacock, colleague D. A. Pennebaker, and others are preparing a series of television films that may eventually be seen in theaters as well. The above frame from one of these films, a study of Latin America's reaction to Fidel Castro, shows a mother and child in Venezuela— and demonstrates that Leacock's eye for the beautiful image remains as sharp as ever.*

BERT STERN, one of the most handsomely rewarded magazine and advertising photographers in the United States, hankered at the age of 29 for something more. Gathering a sizeable crew and sum (eventually $210,000 was needed), he set off for the Newport (R.I.) Jazz Festival in 1959 to shoot his first film, the 81-minute Jazz on a Summer's Day. *With no special knowledge of jazz, Stern approached his subject mainly through the faces of the musicians and spectators, using up to six cameras simultaneously to record performances by, among others, Gerry Mulligan and Louis Armstrong (above, left and right). Cutting back and forth between shots of performers, audience, the town itself, and the America Cup races then in progress offshore (center), the film evokes in exquisite, sometimes funny, often lyrical images the sound and color of Newport Jazz.*

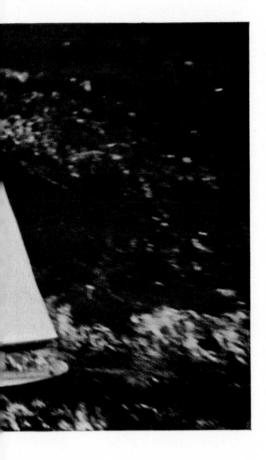

TEXT CONTINUED FROM PAGE 13

Thompson's *N.Y., N.Y.*, pictured on pages 12 and 13) to a documentary look at the spiritually dispossessed of Los Angeles (Sidney Meyers's *The Savage Eye,* page 14).

Perhaps the true common denominator among the artists on these pages is a belief that the film is *the* art form of our time. Throughout the world young intellectuals have hungrily studied the work of the cinema's early masters in search of inspiration. Besides a passion for movies, these particular eight living in New York have in common a bent for nonconformity and a strong personal stamp on their work. Although movie making is group enterprise, their films are essentially the embodied idea of one individual. Jonas Mekas, editor of *Film Culture,* spokesman for the current New York film movement, and now himself a film maker, has appropriated for them the French New Wave's phrase for the same kind of movie—"an author's cinema."

In New York the work of Morris Engel greatly affected young film makers. His full-length films (*The Little Fugitive*, 1953; *Lovers and Lollipops*, 1955; *Weddings and Babies,* 1957) have been acknowledged by François Truffaut (maker of *The 400 Blows*) as one of the most significant influences on France's New Wave—which in turn stimulated New York's. Although Engel prefers not to be grouped with the other film makers discussed here—he thinks of himself as an advanced maker of commercial features—he has led the way in films of spontaneity and naturalness. His experiments with highly portable camera and sound systems have had a profound effect on New York film technique by showing how to move in and capture unrehearsed situations far removed from the studio.

After Engel's second picture, the next impetus was felt with Lionel Rogosin's provocative *On the Bowery* (1956). The real surge was under way when John Cassavetes made *Shadows* (1959). On its heels followed *Pull My Daisy;* and it was this film, along with *Come Back, Africa; The Savage Eye;* and *Jazz on a Summer's Day*—all released in 1960—that made critics realize a new tide was rising. —ELIZABETH SUTHERLAND

By SANTHA RAMA RAU

In Search of Paradise

A world traveler takes a hard look at the Shangri-La's

of the shrinking globe and finds that a few endure

The Red Fort at Delhi

"The Great Moguls! Those words sound to-day like the title of some old Oriental fairy story, like the name of some legend. . . . Behind the . . . ramparts of Delhi the Great Moguls had another enchanted palace even more magnificent than the one at Agra. The great pointed arches of the Delhi palace look on to a garden shut in by high and crested walls. The splendour of the delicate structure has never been exceeded, but it is a prison if only for fairies and genii. What need to say that it is of the whitest marble, or that the ceilings rain their frosted icicles upon the matchless carvings? But here masses of gold mingle with the whiteness of the marble, and their colours blend into a new harmony. The thousand wondrously chiselled arabesques lining the walls and roof appear in a setting of sparkling gold. No other light but that which comes through the arches opening on to the garden enters the palace, so that the columns and indented arches which succeed each other in a diminishing perspective appear to fade into a thin blue haze, yet all the roofs and walls seem to have the transparency of alabaster." PIERRE LOTI: *India*

"If there is a paradise on earth, it is here, it is here, it is here." "Here" was one of the great halls of the Red Fort in Old Delhi where one can still see the decorative Persian script of the seventeenth century illuminating these words over the arches. The Grand Mogul, Shah Jehan, who reigned from the jewel-encrusted peacock throne and at whose command the whole complex of pavilions and palaces, of exquisite mosques, rose-filled gardens, lotus pools, and waterfalls were built on the edge of the Jumna river, might well have thought his lavish court a paradise on earth. If you go there now, you can hardly help admiring the elegance and delicacy of the architecture in the Red Fort. You may, however, find the high crenelated sandstone walls surrounding the whole Mogul center somewhat forbidding, an uncomfortable reminder of the dangers that threatened that "paradise." Looking out from the terraces, you will see that the Jumna has changed its course in the last couple of hundred years, and your view will be of a wide, undistinguished plain, dotted here and there with clusters of ramshackle huts. On the city side of the walls there will be the usual mess of crowded Indian bazaars, impromptu wooden stalls, the poor and crowded life of the streets. No longer really a paradise.

All the same, the idea of a paradise on earth seems to be deeply a part of people's imagination and longing, a place where life is easy, untroubled, fulfilling, where the people are friendly, beautiful, intelligent, kind, where nature and climate are bountiful and not forces to be subdued like an enemy, a place one never wants to leave. To meet these requirements people have, from time

21

to time, described imaginary lands—Utopia, Atlantis, Shangri-La (somewhat offset, of course, by such books as *Brave New World* or *1984*)—and a great many lucky, adventurous, or distracted souls have by choice or accident set out to find their own paradise in real places. Some of them have even been happy and satisfied there—Paul Gauguin in Tahiti, Lafcadio Hearn in Kyoto, or even, in a less rhapsodic way, Bernard Berenson in Florence. But a great many people have, like Gauguin, a more romantic, less accessible place as their dream setting. If you ask them to describe their imagined place of escape, it is likely to be an island, a tropical island (few people seem to pick mountain fastnesses or inland retreats). Another factor that carries remarkable power is the magic of names, remote, exotic, enchanted—Zanzibar, Zamboanga, Mandalay, the Nicobars, the Seychelles, Celebes—all much more stimulating in sound than, say, Smithville.

Edward Lear, for instance, wrote his wonderfully lilting lines, "On the Coast of Coromandel, Where the early pumpkins blow . . ." and was later echoed by Edith Sitwell, more fantastically, "On the Coast of Coromandel, Dancing to the tunes of Handel. . . ." The reality is less pleasingly strange and bewitching. The Coromandel Coast is a long, barren stretch north of Madras in India. It is dry, grillingly hot, enlivened only by small impoverished villages and some scraggly coconut, toddy, and areca palms. Even though Mr. Lear's impassioned Yonghy-Bonghy-Bo in his desperate courtship of Lady Jingly assured her that "shrimps and watercresses" grow in profusion along his Coromandel Coast, still, I know from prosaic experience that the best shrimp are found on India's west coast (which has no romantic name) and salad needs a cooler, moister climate.

In the course of a good deal of traveling about during the last twenty years of my life, I have had occasion to visit or live in a number of places that have at one time or another been considered paradises. It is often a chastening experience. Fashions in paradises change, and in the past couple of decades the war and, later, quick and simple travel have destroyed much of the romance and much of the exclusiveness of such standard dream props as the "South Sea Islands," the "Indies," the "Spice Islands." Another more pedestrian reason for the change is that the ranks of the travelers are greatly swollen these days by a different sort of person—exchange students, earnest workers on foundation grants, sociologists, anthropologists, journalists, and so on. They haven't, I think, quite the paradise mentality. After all, the requirements are pretty rare nowadays: a private unearned income or a job that keeps you in a remote foreign place for years together, and a consuming interest that can be pursued there to temper a sense of boredom, and no desire whatever to return home. The beachcomber grows exceedingly rare.

History, recent and ancient, has justified some paradises and discredited others. Capri, which held the love and imagination of Norman Douglas has, according to more re-

cent visitors, fallen into the hands of the blue jeans and sandals set and might as well be East Hampton for all the inaccessible charm it now commands. The Aegean Islands, however, retain the glamour and strength that drew a Byron to them. The Italian coastal village that cost Shelley his life is now a tacky little resort fronted by beach hotels, many of them named for him. But then, again, Robert Graves still lives in Majorca, and Paul Bowles is still infatuated with Tangiers, even though, for a while, he owned an odd and pleasing island in the lovely bay of Weligama in south Ceylon. There he lived in an octagonal house built by an eccentric French furniture manufacturer. It was surrounded by tangled romantic gardens dropping suddenly away to miniature rocky harbors and could only be reached on foot across a sandbank that appeared at low tide.

One can still read an author like Maria Dermoût, who, in her two beautifully written books, *The Ten Thousand Things* and *Yesterday*, captures both the dream and the life of those distant days in the Indies which were both delightful and profitable for the Dutch. Here is almost a classic description of the conventional paradise:

And as the days were all the same, so were the years. . . . Sunlight and dust and hot vibrating skies, hazy days, short twilights, and the long clear tropical nights full of cool mountain wind and moon and stars. To the south the Southern Cross over the rustling trees, looking like a kite on its side, and overhead Orion, big and powerful. Delicate bamboo foliage etched against the sky; silver palm leaves washed with moonlight and waving like fans, slowly and gracefully in the night. A whispering wind.

Significantly, her stories are set more than fifty years ago. Indonesian independence hasn't changed the scenery, but it has put an end to the kind of life she describes. Joseph Conrad, however, who knew the same part of the world well, was ahead of his time in this matter and foreshadowed the disillusion that paradises were to bring to many people over the years. To me, the most chillingly moving passages of *An Outcast of the Islands* are the moments when Willems surveys the dreary prospect of the village in which he must spend the rest of his life. All the correct requisites are there—the beautiful girl who loves him with undiminished ardor, the charming palm-thatched houses, the lush tropical landscape—yet all he can see is that the exuberant green all around him will never pale with the springtime, never yellow with autumn, will always remain this same green, that this undemanding life will go on and on and nothing will ever happen to him until he dies. In a way, it is a life sentence.

The other moment of the book that took on a quite startling reality for me when I was on a visit to Makassar, the capital of Celebes (now Sulawesi), was the description of Almayer's decaying office: the jumble of books that someone had once planned to read, the moldering files, the tepid effort at order by a man who had already forgotten the purpose of such an effort or its meaning. Today, Celebes—shaped, the Indonesians tell you with great charm, like an orchid—has a capital that reflects in a larger way the penalties of living in the outposts of a reputed paradise. Makassar is a drab, damp town, undistinguished by architecture of either novelty or beauty. Its hotel, grandly called the Grand, serves only to remind you that there must once have been another, gayer life here, that planters and spice merchants must at one time have come down from their estates and spice gardens upcountry (surrounded by friendly and beautiful natives) to spend an evening dancing in the hotel ballroom. It is almost never used now. The piano is locked, the band platform covered with dust; the walled gardens outside, filled with frangipani and trellised arcades, are untidy, spotted with cushions of moss between the flagstones. The old Dutch Fort down the street with its high lichened walls must once have sent out dashing young officers to dance with the pretty daughters, the sedate wives, to stroll with them along the sea wall and watch the flaming sunset and the return of the square-sailed fishing boats.

Now Fort Rotterdam is occupied by Indonesian soldiers, sensibly dressed in khaki, whose job it is to cope with the trouble from the tribes upcountry. The hotel is virtually deserted. When I was there my fellow guests were a couple of Chinese families, a couple of administrative officials, a few soberly dressed Indonesian businessmen. The dining room still presented elaborate menus in Dutch and English, but the waiters didn't bother to set more than half a dozen tables because most people knew that they could get a far better meal by buying oddments off the stalls in the bazaar. The colonial life is gone, and so are the oases of calm and comfort and delight that foreigners found there.

Walking by on the streets, the people of Makassar still wear their brilliant silk sarongs in fuchsia, aquamarine, gold, and the women still cover their heads with filmy shawls of muslin and lace, and powder their faces an arresting dead white for beauty—a graceful, withdrawn people. But what would one *do* living there?—the problem in many paradises. Watch the shifting light on the beautiful expanse of Makassar Bay? Drive in a pony cart tinkling with small bells past the brick factory, past the suburban houses, to a glimpse of the countryside? Watch a football game on the soggy playing fields? I once asked a pedicab driver what was the best thing to do in Makassar. He answered at once, "You must go to the Sirène, that is the best." It sounded exotic enough, even slightly wicked. It turned out to be a whitewashed concrete movie house showing an old Indian film. The driver could not understand why the excursion did not fill me with enthusiasm.

Something of the same sort of depression overcame me when I went to Zamboanga on the far western peninsula of Mindanao, in the southern Philippines. I had always heard that the place held such attraction that girls used to sing to their navy sweethearts, "Don't you go, don't you go to far Zamboanga"—it would certainly be the end of the romance because the women of Zamboanga and the place itself were

so lovely that any man would be captivated forever. This legend is rather hard to believe since the Japanese occupation and the equally devastating effect of the American return have changed the look and the atmosphere of the town. Even the multicolored sands, once the glory of the Zamboanga beaches and described to me by a Filipino friend as "fragments of rubies, emeralds, sapphires, thrown away by some mad jeweler," seemed to me an almost uniform charcoal gray. True, the sleepy accommodating air of the town is still there; true, the Moslem traders still stand beside their magnificent painted boats and bargain for spices on the quayside, but the war did more than destroy the pretty wooden houses and the warm prosperity of Zamboanga. It ruined a dream, and it is now hard to think of the tidy postwar housing, the wide concrete highway leading to the airstrip, the neat little squares flanked by administrative buildings, and shops selling souvenirs as the correct backdrop for a paradise.

I suppose that among the few paradises I have lived in which match their reputation—and indeed go beyond it—the most appealing is Bali. That small island off the coast of Java—only a tiny particle of the great, graceful curve of islands cutting across the Equator that make up Indonesia—retains a character, a life, a marvelous spell of its own that changes constantly but never disappears. Change, in fact, is what most people who have known and loved Bali seem to fear most. In their writings and their talk, their reminiscences, even their painting, they seem to assure you continually that Bali was perfect when they knew it; any alteration must be for the worse. In my opinion, and as the result of three different stays in Bali that my husband and I have spread over twelve years, it is precisely this element of change, of continuing invention and excitement—the recognition of boredom—that has kept Bali a paradise when other more static ways of life and attitude have faded.

*S*ome years ago Beryl de Zoete, the English commentator on the dance, described "the curious spectacle, fascinating in its absurdity," of a traditional Balinese dance interspersed with comic episodes in which the dancers wear spectacles, an Inverness cape, a feathered American Indian headdress, and other surrealist gear. This leads her to comment: "The Balinese, deprived of his tradition, seems to have no style at all." To me such a performance seems only an aspect of the Balinese sense of fun and ludicrousness and a continual joy in innovation. If Miss De Zoete were to go to Bali now, she probably wouldn't see anything like the same dance, although some Balinese dance group may well have tried to do some other dance in, perhaps, Chinese silks or straw hats just for amusement or to see how it would look. Some of their experiments will stick—the girls in a popular dance called the *janger* still wear an imitation of a Russian ballerina's crown, but made out of fresh flowers—others will vanish as their appeal loses its novelty. But the sense of change, while disturbing to the paradise-seeker, is, I think, essential to the vitality of the paradise.

Bali can, however, offer more traditional qualities: a ravishing landscape—hillsides terraced with great glassy steps of flooded rice fields or the vibrant green of the young shoots, the pine forests and lakes in the hills in the center of the island, the pale sandy beaches, the palms, the mild, pleasing climate, the hedges climbing with bougainvillaea and hibiscus. But most of all, the Balinese people, who have all the charm and physical beauty of the paradise-inhabitants of one's most extravagant imagination, still retain a strong and stimulating personality of their own. They are far from "simple natives." Their arts are much too advanced to be called "delightfully primitive." They are eminently civilized, but with no desire to emulate the West. Once I asked a Balinese friend if he never wished to travel abroad. He replied that he *had* traveled. He had been to Java (only a few miles from his island), and what he saw there was enough to convince him that Bali was the best place in the world.

A great many foreigners who have at one time or another lived in or visited Bali would be inclined to agree with him. Vicki Baum wrote one of her best novels, *A Tale From Bali*, in deep sympathy with a moment of its splendid, almost incredible history, a moment of bewildered heartbreak when the Balinese were called on to fight their first "war." The invading Dutch decided to take over Bali (only about fifty years ago) and sailed their soldier-laden ships up to the coast. The young Balinese men, seeing this amazing arrival, met it in the only way that seemed proper to them. They

TEXT CONTINUED ON PAGE 31

MAX TATCH—SHOSTAL

Capri

"Far aloft on the great rock was pitched . . . the amazing creation of the friend who had offered me hospitality, and whom I envied the privilege of being able to reward a heated, artless pilgrim with a revelation of effects so incalculable. There was none but the loosest prefigurement as the creaking and puffing little boat, which had conveyed me only from Sorrento, drew closer beneath the prodigious island—beautiful, horrible, and haunted—that does most, of all the happy elements and accidents, towards making the Bay of Naples, for the study of composition, a lesson in the grand style. There was only, above and below, through the blue of the air and sea, a great confused shining of hot cliffs and crags and buttresses, a loss, from nearness, of the splendid couchant outline and the more comprehensive mass, and an opportunity—oh, not lost, I assure you—to sit and meditate, even moralise, on the empty deck, while a happy brotherhood of American and German tourists, including, of course, many sisters, scrambled down into little waiting, rocking tubs, and, after a few strokes, popped systematically into the small orifice of the Blue Grotto. There was an appreciable moment when they were all lost to view in that receptacle, the daily "psychological" moment during which it must so often befall the recalcitrant observer on the deserted deck to find himself aware of how delightful it might be if none of them should come out again."

HENRY JAMES:
The Art of Travel

Capri can claim distinction as the oldest fashionable resort in the Western world. Opposite: One of the imperial Romans who first "discovered" it gazes down upon the eastern tip of the island and, across the bay, the port of Sorrento. If Henry James thought Capri overrun by tourists in 1900, he should see it now. At the left is a marine traffic jam located at the entrance to the Blue Grotto.

Kyoto

KATO—F.P.G.

"The first impression received after passing the gate is that of a grand old English park: the colossal trees, the shorn grass, the broad walks, the fresh sweet scent of verdure, all awaken English memories. But as you proceed farther these memories are slowly effaced, and the true Oriental impression defines: you perceive that the forms of those mighty trees are not European; various and surprising exotic details reveal themselves; and then you are gazing down upon a sheet of water containing high rocks and islets connected by bridges of the strangest shapes. Gradually—only gradually—the immense charm, the weird Buddhist charm of the place, grows and grows upon you; and the sense of its vast antiquity defines to touch that chord of the aesthetic feeling which brings the vibration of awe."   LAFCADIO HEARN:
Gleanings in Buddha-fields

Kyoto was founded in A.D. 794 by the Emperor Kwammu, who called it "city of peace" (Heian-kyo). It was for eleven centuries the seat of the government. Adorned with many exquisite gardens, shrines, and temples, it is the center of Buddhism in Japan. The arch in the picture at right is one of many ancient torii, *the majestic gateways to Shinto shrines.*

Tahiti

". . . the beauteous nymph, Fayaway . . . was my peculiar favourite. Her free, pliant figure was the very perfection of female grace and 'beauty. . . . Her hair of the deepest brown, parted irregularly in the middle, flowed in natural ringlets over her shoulders, and whenever she chanced to stoop, fell over and hid from view her lovely bosom. . . . The easy unstudied graces of a child of Nature like this, breathing from infancy an atmosphere of perpetual summer, and nurtured by the simple fruits of the earth, enjoying a perfect freedom from care and anxiety, and removed effectually from all injurious tendencies, strike the eye in a manner which cannot be portrayed. . . . Though in my eyes, at least, Fayaway was indisputably the loveliest female I saw in Typee, yet the description I have given of her will in some measure apply to nearly all the youthful portion of her sex in the valley. Judge ye then, reader, what beautiful creatures they must have been."

HERMAN MELVILLE:
Typee

The two Tahitian girls in the picture opposite are seated on the bank of a pool near the celebrated waterfall of Fatua.

Isfahan

"By far the most lovely thing I saw in Isfahan was the Madrasseh, meaning school; but if a school at all, then a school for pensiveness, for contemplation, for spiritual withdrawal. . . . One is allowed to be lonely there; but in more civilised communities no one is allowed to be lonely; the refinement of loneliness is not understood. Was it the mere visual beauty of the place that produced this profound impression? . . . aware that I was all too apt to be led astray by such outward seductions, I examined my impressions severely . . . a long range of buildings, tiled in blue, enclosed a rectangular space; a long pool, with steps going down into the water, reflected the buildings; lilac and irises . . . seemed but a deeper echo of the colours of the tiles; a golden light of sunset struck the white trunks of the plane trees . . . and among the lilacs, the irises, and the planes strolled the tall, robed figures, or sat by the water's edge, idly stirring the water with the point of a stick, so that the reflections quivered to a cloud of amethyst and blue, then steadied again to mirror in glassy stillness the blue walls, the spreading leaves, the evening sky."

V. SACKVILLE-WEST:
Passenger to Teheran

The ancient capital of Persia was adorned by Shah Abbas I with a layout of mosques, gardens, and fountains so magnificent that, as the Persian proverb proclaims: "Half the world is Isfahan." The court of the Madrasseh is at left.

Bali

"This gentleness pervades all Balinese life. They regard and converse with natural objects as they would with friends. I have seen a man about to climb a lontar tree, but before doing so he spoke to it in soothing tones, then embraced it. Finally he climbed, having, so to speak, obtained its consent. . . . The final effect of Bali is harmony: a life undisturbed by the cosmic reflections to no purpose that hound us in the rest of the world. Such problems are settled for them by a consoling religion developed especially for them. What is the result? . . . the effect upon the people, and upon him who comes to see, is one of moving along with the feet just off the ground in an atmosphere of sparkling, brilliant colour." HENDRIK DE LEEUW:
Crossroads of the Java Sea

Thatched huts and cultivated terraces blend perfectly with the luxuriant landscape of Bali, as on the opposite page.

Kashmir

"Kashmir is like rest when the day's work is done. There I led a life of complete idleness. Day after day I lay back among the red-embroidered cushions of my 'shikara' while the boatmen plied their heart-shaped oars along the Jhelum River where fragrant bushes dip their blossoms into the water and banks run up to meet fields of mustard. Sometimes we sped across the waters of Lak Dal to some pleasure garden of the Great Moguls. On every side the towering snow peaks of the Himalayas encircled the 'Happy Valley' as if to shut off that bit of Paradise from the turmoil of the rest of the world. . . . On other days the Shalimar, 'The Abode of Love,' saw my 'shikara' moored for long hours beneath its walls while I wandered where once the beautiful Nourmahal, 'Light of the Harem,' of Jehangir, laughed and loved and danced beside the same fountains that played for me. Surely they sang: "Pale hands I loved beside the Shalimar. Where are you now? . . ."

HENRIETTA SANDS MERRICK:
In the World's Attic

For all the conquerors of India—Afghan, Mogul, as well as British—Kashmir has been a Himalayan refuge from the summer heat. Ringed by the mountains of Afghanistan, China, and Tibet, the Vale of Kashmir is the creation of the Jhelum River which flows through the valley to the northwest, widening here and there to form mirror lakes such as the one shown opposite. Boats on the Jhelum River, once the only reliable means of travel in Kashmir, are now a mainstay of the tourist trade, as shown at right.

TEXT CONTINUED FROM PAGE 24

dressed themselves up in their scarlet and gold finery, tucked hibiscus flowers into their headbands, marched to the beaches in a fantastic glittering procession, set themselves in dance poses—each with his ceremonial kris drawn. When the Dutch opened fire and some of the brave and elegant youths died in the sand, the rest of the Balinese "army" turned their krises on themselves in one of the strangest mass suicides in history. Perhaps it is the first recorded passive resistance movement.

But the Balinese coped with colonialism as they have with Westernization (bicycles and cars on the island), with industrialization (a canning factory opened by a Chinese), with changing politics. Communists, for instance, have tried to convert them, have set up an office in the small city of Denpasar, and have been treated with the unfailing courtesy of the people. After months of campaigning and propaganda, only two Balinese had been enlisted, both known to their own people as chronic malcontents. However, when the Communists' effort was stopped because the Balinese were not "prepared" for these new theories, both the young men were reaccepted, without drama, into their society.

Is Bali still a paradise? Yes, if you are willing to move with the Balinese as they move, without retaining what I call a "museum mentality," without insisting that things should be preserved as they were when you first loved them, crystallized in time and space and memory.

After Bali, few other paradises quite meet their reputations. It is hard to believe, for instance, that the Emperor Babur, the first of the great Moguls to invade India, whose ancestral domain included the fabulous city of Samarkand, pined always for Kabul. In those days perhaps Kabul really was "the orchard of Asia" or, alternatively, "the garden of Asia." Certainly he found it a strong contrast with India, which according to his memoirs had "no skill or knowledge

EWING KRAININ

in design or architecture . . . no grapes or musk-melons, no good fruits, no ice or cold water, no good food, or bread in their bazaars, no baths or colleges, no candles, no torches, not a candlestick." It is true that in this disagreeable land he laid out the splendid capital of Agra, which his descendants later embellished with the Taj Mahal, Fatehpursikri, and the great Agra Fort, but he never wished to stay there and never regretted the place that his great-great-grandson was to describe as a "paradise on earth." He yearned always for the "melons, grapes, and flowers" of Kabul, and asked only to be buried there when he died.

Well, go to Kabul now. You will find a scruffy little town, proud of its one paved road (built by the Russians from the airport, past the foreign embassies, to the center of town, for the arrival of Khrushschev in Afghanistan some years ago). All around is a tangle of muddy alleys and crowded bazaars; open drains carry refuse down to the opaque, dirty river that cuts through the town. The streets are a crush of miscellaneous traffic: horse carts, rickshaws, the few motorcars of foreigners and cabinet ministers, and pedestrians either encased in the tentlike Moslem *bourkhous* or wearing the striped, sashed robes of the men. A little way out of town you can find carefully cultivated private gardens (walled against the public view) and, beyond, the lovely jade-green hills that surround Kabul, the apple orchards that fill the spring with blossoms. These must have been what Babur was dreaming of, for no one could now describe Kabul itself as beautiful, charming, or even quaint. Yet it must have changed a great deal; for Babur, who had trekked across the magnificence of the Himalayas, who had seen Kashmir in its flood of dramatic beauty, was consumed with homesickness for what is now an ugly, provincial town.

Later emperors, however, found themselves entranced with the magic of Kashmir, and that, even though it is not an island, and not tropical, remains a paradise of a sort. A well-explored paradise, admittedly, but still, hundreds of expatriate Englishmen and thousands of Indians have found it the place of their dreams, beginning with its most devoted fan, the Emperor Jehangir, who constructed the famous gardens of Shalimar and Nishat Bagh and went there every year. Not literally, but in a sense, Kashmir *is* an island, a bright green valley carpeted in spring with mustard flowers and purple iris, filled with flowering trees later, dense with the summer green of chenar trees and the fiery colors of autumn as the year progresses, all encircled with the towering snows of the highest mountains in the world.

Caught in this small theater of extraordinary scenery and diverse climate are a race of beautiful (but poor), accommodating (but canny), talented (but hidebound) people. Like the Balinese they have their special and distinctive arts —wood carving, embroidery, the making of Kashmir's famous shawls, elaborately chased and hammered silverware, lacquerwork in ancient Mogul designs—but unlike the Balinese their arts are not an evanescent expression of a joy or experience of life, dancing, music, theater. They don't perform much, they *make*. And they seldom use the things they make—those are for the rich or the outsiders to buy.

Life is harder for them, and I think it expresses itself in this way. Yet, captivated by Kashmir's beauty and its gentle pace of life, many foreigners have settled there. A number are, of course, retired British civil servants or army officers who, after their long tour of duty, can no longer imagine living in the chillier social and physical climates of the West. Others are artists, writers, even one carpet designer that I knew who had set up a business with local craftsmen. Most of them were both dismayed and astonished when the trouble between Pakistan and India flared up in their precious valley. One of them, Gerald Hanley—an excellent English novelist who had so adopted Kashmir that he had married a Kashmiri girl and planned his writing future from Kashmir—remarked to me, "It's a great bore. I suppose we must all now go trailing off to find some *other* perfect place to live."

The other perfect places get fewer and fewer. Nevertheless, the exigencies of modern life have in their own way produced one or two new kinds of paradise. The Channel Islands —Jersey, Guernsey, Herm, Alderney, Sark—with their special position compounded of accessibility from England and remoteness (in character), have often provided a haven for individuals in the grand tradition of European eccentrics. Victor Hugo, for instance, when he had to leave France for attacking Louis Napoleon, went to live in Jersey. There he rashly criticized Queen Victoria and had to move to Guernsey, which proved more tolerant and allowed him to settle down in peace to the writing of *Les Miserables* and *Toilers of the Sea*. George Eliot and Swinburne both found sanctuary in the islands. T. H. White lives a solitary life in Alderney, writing about King Arthur's court, studying and practicing falconry, and raising dogs. Prince von Blücher used to hold the tiny island of Herm where, for reasons he never cared to disclose, he raised Australian wallabies. Sir Compton Mackenzie, who took over the Crown lease to Herm later on, raised cats in extravagant numbers. People who went to visit him there still describe with a kind of nervous wonder the sight of his thin, erect figure striding down to meet the boat, followed by a great procession of many-colored cats.

Now, however, the wallabies are all gone and the cats sadly reduced in number under the regime of the present tenant. But it still retains its rather threatening beauty and an air of independence that is impressed even on the postcard-buying tourist when he finds that Herm, with its three hundred acres of land and its half-dozen families, still insists on issuing its own local stamps.

From either Herm or Guernsey, none of the other islands in the Channel haunts you, at least visually, in quite so persistent a way as Sark. Others are bigger or smaller or prettier in the mists of the sea, but Serk, Sark, Serq (however you spell it) is constantly in your consciousness, catching your eye in any seascape, lurking like a half-submerged hippopotamus in any view from the harbor or the hilltops. Other islanders are apt to describe it as "all wind and visitors," but it has seemed to countless foreigners the most magnetic of the islands.

The boats to Sark are at best irregular and often run only once each week or ten days because in high winds or heavy seas it is impossible to land in Sark's minute harbor. From the sea it is forbiddingly austere; a three-hundred-foot rise to the plateau forms the hippopotamus's back, and all around the cliffs are honeycombs of caves and grottoes. But beyond the harbor, Sark is unexpectedly lovely, cut by wooded valleys, studded by miniature heaths brilliant with yellow gorse, filled with the sound of wind and sea. The five hundred people who live on Sark guard the silence and privacy of their island, but it has acquired a rather special renown and attraction partly because it maintains one of the strangest, most inexplicable governments in the world, partly because the Sarkees pay no income tax, partly because the climate is mild and sunny. The combination makes it an almost irresistible paradise to well-off, tradition-minded Britons.

*T*he Dame of Sark is an elderly woman called Mrs. Sybil Hathaway, who inherited the title and the Crown rights to Sark from her grandmother. As something between an administrator and a sovereign, she rules the island through a complex series of archaic laws, family rights, and personal whims. By tradition, for instance, she is the only person permitted to keep pigeons on Sark because pigeon pie was a delicacy reserved for the family of the *seigneurie*—the traditional seigneurs or dames of the island. Equally, only the Dame may own a bitch. The reason for this seems to be rather more mysterious, possibly just an alarming rise in the dog population. A recent regulation prohibits any sort of automobile because the Dame feels the exhaust fumes might pollute the air. No one can come to live on Sark without her approval, and she can, if she wishes, expel a resident.

Beyond these rather bizarre rights the Dame of Sark has virtually complete authority in the government through the Sarkee Parliament. However, the Sarkees don't seem to resent these privileges. They remind you that, on occasion, the assumption of authority by the Dame is an excellent quality. When the Germans landed on Sark in the last war, the story goes, they sent an officer up to the Dame's castle to commandeer it for German billets. She is said to have received the officer in her study and to have remained seated, according to the rights of her rank, while the officer was kept standing, according to his position as an inferior. She returned a cool refusal to his request, and when he remarked, "You do not seem to be afraid of the German army," she is supposed

to have replied, "I have not had occasion to expect discourtesy from a gentleman." Whether it was the force of her personality or a change in German plans, the fact is that apart from building a few defenses against commando attacks, the Sarkees were left alone.

As Sark's reputation has soared with the needs of modern life, other small paradises have lost the attractions they once held. Zanzibar, for example, though it still carries the associations of the old days of spice trading, though you can still, if the wind is right, smell the fragrance of cloves from a mile out to sea, is not really a place of romance, adventure, escape, any more. Carefully tended palm groves and clove gardens provide the island with a healthy income. Narrow streets winding through the old quarter, where pedestrians have to flatten themselves against the walls when an automobile passes, and great brass-studded carved wooden doors leading to impenetrable houses provide atmosphere for the visitor while innumerable small shops filled with souvenirs and GENUINE Zanzibar chests delight the shopper. The Arab dhows still sail into the harbor; the white, spacious administrative buildings with their airy galleries still line the shore; the hotel is a converted Arab house laced with tortuous corridors and unexpected stairways (and air conditioning). In short, Zanzibar is a tourist's paradise—a very different thing from a *real* paradise.

Much closer to a *real* paradise is the south coast of the island of Ceylon, scalloped with perfect beaches, fringed with coconut palms, and beyond, the emerald sea stretching all the way to Antarctica. In all of that lovely coast my favorite place is the small walled port of Galle. There, I was once told, "The fish in the market are the color of rubies, and you can buy cinnamon stick by the yard." There are also the storybook splendors of the East. Old men sit in open workshops polishing cloudy piles of moonstones and opals, sorting glittering displays of sapphires, white zircons, Matara diamonds, fashioning elaborate combs and hairpins from silver and tortoise shell studded with brilliants. Devil dancers, festivals, slow-moving masked dramas are part of your daily life. The swift leap of a catamaran over the breakers out to sea, the easygoing Singhalese nature, the magnificent ruins of a past civilization in the central hills—all these offer variety, excitement, and contentment to your life in Ceylon. Perhaps the best clue to its special appeal is in the infinitely provocative names that successive waves of foreigners—the Greeks, Moors, Tamils, Portuguese, Dutch—have given to the island: Taprobane, Tenerisim, Ilinare, Hibenard, Serendib, or Isle of Spices, Pearl of the Indian Ocean, Isle of Delight. . . .

A *real* paradise must be as heady as its name.

Santha Rama Rau was born in India, reared and educated in the United States and England. She is an inveterate traveler and has written books on Japan and Russia as well as India.

"My monastery,"

says France's greatest architect,

"descends from the heavens,

touching the earth only where it must"

CORBUSIER'S CLOISTER

Le Corbusier's new monastery of La Tourette is a massive hollow cube of rough reinforced concrete thrust out from the brow of a gentle hill (right). The upper two stories are ringed on three sides with the projecting balconies of the monks' cells (interior view, above). Lower down, behind the rhythmic concrete sunbreakers, are common rooms and the refectory. And in the court, along with a cross-shaped series of cloister passageways, one finds such typical innovations as the small cube-and-pyramid oratory for student monks (at top).

By CRANSTON JONES

Rearing up from the rolling French farmlands of Eveux-sur-Arbresle, some sixteen miles outside Lyon, there stands today a massive monastery in raw concrete unlike any church structure ever seen before, but one that has already become a three-star stop on any modern architecture tour of Europe. In fact, Le Couvent Sainte-Marie de la Tourette had become a shrine for architectural pilgrimages even before it was formally dedicated by the Dominican Master General from Rome last September. This is patently not due to its beauty; the structure is almost purposefully brutal, angular, and unfinished, with the marks of the wooden framework into which the concrete was poured left nakedly and unabashedly exposed (and as such, a prime example of what architects are now calling "the new brutalism"). Its uppermost rows of projecting monks' cells seem to hearken back to the monks'

caves at Mt. Athos; its slab-sided church walls of gray concrete with the curious free-form chapel suggest grim coastal artillery bunkers.

Yet this powerful, looming structure projecting out from the brow of the hill has been unhesitatingly called "overwhelming" by architects fortunate enough to visit it. Paris's distinguished *Le Monde* has commented that this monastery "moulded in a modern crust and in modern forms evokes the spirit and recovers the forces of the monasteries of the Middle Ages." The critic of *La Croix* has gone even further, saying that the masterful hand of the architect is everywhere so apparent that even when centuries have passed and only a crumbling wall remains, it will identify the artist: "Le Corbusier constructs the celebrated ruins of the fortieth century."

A good deal of the excitement generated in European

The bold angles of the bell tower (above) evoke a cubist sculpture of a giant hand flung aloft, although one of the monks has likened it to a medieval bell tower, "powerful and austere, with a note of humor." The monastery roof (opposite, above) has been walled and sown with grass to make a secluded "cloister." Less restful is the inner court (opposite, below) where the welter of geometric forms approaches confusion.

architectural circles by this new building derives from the fact that the architect is Le Corbusier, by universal consent France's greatest living architect. Indeed, throughout that part of the world where concrete, rather than steel, is the prime building material, he is now heralded as the presiding genius of mid-twentieth-century architecture. Others, of course, would maintain that the late Frank Lloyd Wright's achievements loom far larger; still others, that Chicago's German-born Ludwig Mies van der Rohe or Finland's Alvar Aalto equal and even surpass "Corbu"; but none would deny that his bold hand has written large across the history of modern building.

From his cramped atelier on Paris's Left Bank in the 1920's came plans that in the formative years of modern architecture passed overnight into clichés—neat cubed boxes on stilts, duplex studio living rooms, louvered sunshades. His basic city-planning unit, a massive, block-sized slab set on stilts, became a reality with the United Nations Secretariat building on Manhattan's East River (in the early design stage of which he was the dominant figure) and Marseille's Radiant City (a 1952 superblock apartment house that has been called "the most important single building since World War II"). On the heat-blasted plains of India's Punjab, Le Corbusier has in recent years erected Chandigarh, a dramatic new mid-century city. And the world's other dramatic new capital, Brasília, also falls within his orbit; both its Brazilian architect, Oscar Niemeyer, and its town planner, Lucio Costa, are his devoted followers.

But Le Corbusier's emergence as one of the key figures of the age has been accompanied by a curious metamorphosis, of which the monastery of La Tourette is a fascinating example. For this man, who once proclaimed that a new way of living was foreshadowed by transoceanic steamers and airplanes and was wont to compare the Parthenon and custom-built touring cars in one breath, has in recent years moved in an unexpected new direction; namely, toward massive sculptural shapes in rough concrete that stand at the opposite end of the spectrum from the sleek glass, aluminum, and steel towers so prominent in new cityscapes of American cities. His purposeful turning away from a machine aesthetic is in part the result of circumstance: India's Punjab, for instance, has progressed technologically little beyond the wheelbarrow and concrete mixer, and structural steel is beyond the reach of Chandigarh. Then, the monastery of La Tourette had to be constructed for less than $500,000, at a unit cost so low that it qualified for French government financing reserved for the lowest income housing projects. A reinforcing circumstance is the fact that Le Corbusier is at

heart an artist (he devotes half his working day to painting and sculpture). Increasingly, it is the sculptural qualities, rather than fine finish, that have absorbed his attention. *"Avec des matières brutes, établir les rapports émouvants"* ("with brute materials to establish moving relationships") has become his new aim and goal.

Just how Le Corbusier went about creating such *"rapports émouvants"* he himself expounded in an informal speech to the Dominican congregation shortly after the monks took up their abode in the new monastery he designed for them. The late Father Couturier, Dominican middleman between modern artists and the church, who had made possible Matisse's chapel at Vence and Le Corbusier's 1955 pilgrimage chapel at Ronchamp,* had explained to him the steps of the monks' ritual. "Here we walk in double file," he had told the architect. "Here we prostrate ourselves." Le Corbusier next journeyed to the site, sketched the approaches, the horizons, noted the orientation of the sun, and, as he put it, "sniffed out" the topography. "In choosing the place," he says, "I committed the criminal, or the valid act."

"Here," he continued, "in this terrain so mobile, so fluid, so fleeing, plunging, flowing, I said: I am not going to set the foundation on the ground, since it would be lost to sight or else it would cost as much as a Roman or Assyrian fortress. . . . Let us take the foundation on high, from the horizontal of the building at the summit, which will fit it in with the horizon. And, starting from that horizontal on the summit, we will measure everything from there, and we will reach the soil at the moment we touch it. . . . Thus you have a building, very precise at the top, which, little by little, determines its organism as it descends and touches the soil as best it can. It's not something which just anybody could think up. It's an original aspect of this monastery, very original."

It took Le Corbusier and his staff three years to complete the plans. At first he had toyed with the idea of making the grass-seeded roof the cloister, with nothing but heaven above, silence below. "A magnificent cloister," he allowed, "beautiful because you don't see it. You know, with me you'll have paradoxes all the time." But second thoughts set in: "If I put [the cloister] up there it will be so beautiful that the monks will use it for escape, which may imperil their religious life." In the end he did put a promenade area on the roof (see illustration page 37), but he was careful to surround it by high parapets that prevent the brothers from seeing anything but the sky. As he told the Dominicans: "You have a very demanding interior life. The delights of the sky and clouds are perhaps too easy. But go up there from time to time; let them authorize you to go up, a

*Discussed and illustrated in Allan Temko's article, "The Dawn of the High Modern," in HORIZON for September, 1959.

In the inner passageways of La Tourette (opposite) Le Corbusier used rhythmically staggered concrete mullions to create "a drapery of glass." The stone-studded surfaces of the monks' balconies (top) and the water spout (bottom) are other examples of his ability to achieve richness and variety with forms that are resolutely geometrical.

reward for those who have been good boys."

Designing from the top down, Le Corbusier placed one hundred balconied monks' cells on the upper two stories. They are narrow and austere living quarters, each 7 feet 5 inches high (the height of a man standing with arm raised, and Le Corbusier's basic unit of "Modulor" measurement). Below this is a communal floor—library, oratory, classrooms —with the large refectory yet another floor below. Here at mealtime one Dominican reads aloud while the other brothers eat in silence, a huge green curtain drawn to keep out the sun's heat. Linking the areas at what would normally be the cloister level is a cross-shaped pattern of corridors with concrete mullions holding the fixed floor-to-ceiling glass that is staggered in a rhythmic pattern (page 38). As the white-garbed monks move through these areas of austere white concrete (only the doors and overhead water pipes are painted bright primary colors) an extraordinarily moving harmony emerges, one that Le Corbusier clearly anticipated when he predicted that it would only be when the monks took possession that "the architect will speak."

The heart of any monastery is its church for collective services, and its chapel, where individual masses are said each morning. And it is here that Le Corbusier's skill was most profoundly tested. To facilitate an effortless flow of white cowls as the monks enter, ramps lead into the church. Inside, the roof slopes upward to a height of 53 feet over the altar, while the floor descends by platforms and steps. At one side of the church stands the free-form chapel (page 41), which Le Corbusier thinks of as his "rock," and which the monks less reverently call "the ear" because of its convoluted shape. Its bleak, bare concrete forms would be cryptlike without the introduction of outside light and touches of color. Here Le Corbusier's solution has been most ingenious, taking the form of a series of huge light-funnels (which he calls "light cannons") on one side and smaller funnels ("machine guns") on the other. The light, which becomes "tinted" by bright color painted on the interior surfaces of the funnels, is directed primarily at the chapel walls, for Le Corbusier insists that "the emotion comes from what the eyes see, that is the volumes, from which the body receives by the impression or pressure of the walls on itself. . . ."

Le Corbusier sounds almost immodestly gleeful that the large volume of space of his church and chapel has also proven to be acoustically effective ("I am not responsible for it, knowingly . . . but admit that perhaps I have a certain flair . . ."). As to the effectiveness of this space, neither Le Corbusier nor the Dominicans seem in doubt; even in their unfinished state the two sanctuaries emerge as a triumph of Le Corbusier's disciplined and highly plastic three-dimensional vision. "When a work is at its maximum of intensity, of proportion, of quality of execution, of perfection," he points out, "it produces a phenomenon of unutterable space: rooms begin to radiate, physically they shine." This interlocking of disparate elements to create a unified whole which then suddenly bursts forth with a life of its own is, of course, the very test by which a masterpiece distinguishes itself from something simply labeled "a work."

Does the Couvent Sainte-Marie de la Tourette in truth meet such a test? Almost, but not quite. Too many overly geometric solutions (e.g., the cube and pyramid oratory for student monks, on pages 34 and 37) approach a hit-or-miss quality that leaves a spectator uneasily sensing that he is observing a jumble, rather than a great unity. But Le Corbusier, and the monks themselves, have no such doubts. It is significant that the daughter arts of painting and sculpture have not been invited in. "There will be no possible distraction by images," Le Corbusier has ordained, and has made it explicitly clear why he feels there should be none. "If you want to be good fellows and show some feeling for your poor devil of an architect," he has told the monks, "you can do it by formally refusing every gift of stained glass, or images or statues, which kill everything. They are really unnecessary things . . . you must not believe that figurative images of any nature add something if the architecture has created it already." It is a tribute as much to Corbu's persuasiveness as to his architecture that, for the time being at least, the monks are proving obedient to his word.

Cranston Jones is the author of the new book Architecture Today and Tomorrow, *a study of modern architecture through the men who created it. He is an associate editor of* Time.

By WALTER KERR

THE THEATER OF FORM

The playwrights of the nineteen-sixti

As we move with considerable bewilderment and some alarm into the theater of the 1960's, we begin to feel as though we had hold of both ends of one of those firecracker favors that are popular at children's parties. By tugging firmly and simultaneously at the two little tabs—and in opposite directions—you can pull the whole tissue-paper structure apart with a most satisfying *pop!* after which you can rummage in the fragments for a clue to your future.

What tabs—or bears' tails—have we got hold of just now? We are wrenching vigorously, with one clenched fist, to rip the ancient concepts of style and form from the face of our pleasures. Just as vigorously, with the other fist, we are trying to stretch the delights of style and form as far as they may be made to go. Form and anti-form are the opponents of the hour, and the crackle they make as they scratch in passing is apt to become deafening before the party is over.

This tug of war, by the way, does mean to shatter the shape of the theater as we know it, just as the favor disintegrates in a delighted child's hands. It is also a duel to the death: one side means to come out with a longer straw than the other, and never the twain shall be twined again. And it is a contest that is in no sense confined to the theater. In point of fact, my own sharpest awareness of it came not while I was sitting in the playhouse but while I was making my way, fascinated, through a very long short story that was determined *not* to be a short story in *The New Yorker* two years ago.

"I don't dare go anywhere near the short-story form,"

confided J. D. Salinger quite early in his "Seymour, an Introduction." Almost painfully concerned to tell the truth, the whole truth, and nothing but the truth about a brother he'd loved, the author was careful to erase, systematically, every trace of artificial coloring that might have come into being as part of the process of producing literature rather than reality.

Were we in danger of being intrigued by Salinger's own highly personal style? "Woe is me, there's a prose writer in our midst," exclaimed a parenthesis meant to shatter our beginning comfort in the writer's rhythms. Were we being seduced away from the subject and into a love affair with someone's words? "I apologize for that verbiage," intruded another aside, adding, "unfortunately, there's probably more."

Were we in danger of becoming charmed by the progressive dance steps of a sustained narrative? "A day has passed since this last sentence," interrupted the author's voice, calling deliberately disillusioning attention to the presence of the author's hand. "Between the last paragraph and this, just over two and a half months have gone by," warned a further and still more alienating whisper. Not for us the idle amenities of cantering easily along a style-smoothed roadbed beneath a fiction-enriched pattern of sheltering leaves. We must be reminded that a writer is present, and *working*. We must be told that syntax is inadequate to the purposes of truth. We must not be lulled into an illusion of continuity, into mistaking the graces of artful management for the essentially unmanageable presence of life.

AND ANTI-FORM

e tugging from opposite sides at the drama of naturalistic illusion

Reading the piece with that drugged, slow-paced, cocoon-warmed avidity all Salingerers share, I was endlessly haunted by echoes of my theatergoing. For all their buzzing, these were somewhat ambiguous at first. It wasn't until I came to the last column of type that they leaped into formation and began to march forward.

"I'm finished with this," Salinger announced. "Or, rather, it's finished with me. Fundamentally, my mind has always balked at any kind of ending. How many stories have I torn up since I was a boy because they had what that old Chekhov-baiting noise Somerset Maugham calls a Beginning, a Middle, and an End? Thirty-five? Fifty? One of the thousand reasons I quit going to the theater when I was about twenty was that I resented like hell filing out of the theater just because some playwright was forever slamming down his silly curtain. (What ever became of that stalwart bore Fortinbras? Who eventually fixed *his* wagon?) Nonetheless, I'm done here."

What echoes were firmly on the march now? Several thousand, no doubt, if one were to include all one's memories of the plays Chekhov had influenced, the plays Maugham had influenced, and the plays that had begun to take note of a certain restlessness and resentment in the audience that had already had Chekhov and had already had Maugham. But essentially, three.

The first and most easily dismissed of these, of course, is the plainly carpentered, safety-inspected formula play of the twentieth century. It doesn't much matter whether one is thinking of the drawing-room neatness of the second decade (*Our Betters*), the tougher tidiness of the third decade (*The Front Page*), or the sociological orderliness of the post-depression years (*Golden Boy*). All of these specimens are really constructed in the same way, upon the same basic assumptions as to what a play—whatever its content—should look and sound like. The beginning? A tucking-in of unobtrusive but slyly adequate exposition presented as though people were really talking to one another; a casual and plausible laying-in of the plot points. The middle? Our just-folks exposition leads logically, and with no lapses, to something louder though no less natural in the way of a crisis. The end? The crisis scatters a fairish debris about the stage, which debris will be gathered up in a handy dramatic dustpan called The Big Scene or The Big Speech so that the curtain may come down upon an action that has been completed architecturally, rhythmically, and—it would seem—realistically. Given the first twenty minutes of this doll's-house entertainment, you could chart the next two hours with a reasonable accuracy, just as given the locale in the program notes you could always imagine the set.

Not long ago I happened to overhear two theatergoers chatting at random during an intermission. "Do you remember those Big Chief writing tablets," one was asking the other, "with red covers and sheets with blue lines on them?" The other did remember. "Well, they're still making them," announced the first, in a tone of mingled incredulity and triumph. It occurred to me on the spot that most of the three-

43

act, one-set, mark-in-the-exposition and clean-up-the-loose-threads prose plays of the twentieth century seem to have been written on Big Chief tablets. That's what those blue lines were for, to keep the creative hand from straying. It *is* incredible, though not necessarily a triumph, that the formula should have lasted so long; and it is not surprising to know that J. D. Salinger wanted to get out of there, or that Thornton Wilder did get out of there. ("Toward the end of the twenties I began to lose pleasure in going to the theater," Mr. Wilder has said; he'd begun to have a feeling that someone or something had "boxed the action" and "increasingly shut the play up into a museum showcase.") This, of course, is the theater we are now determined to pull apart, to reduce to shreds as the party favor is forever and unregretfully shredded.

But when a man has decided to show his heels to the neat, the plausible, the familiarly shaped, where does he go? If an old formula strikes him as dishonest and unlifelike, what would a new one look like? A playwright may be heartily sick of the theater of naturalistic illusion, of the acted-out pretense that a "slice of life" can really be sliced into precisely weighed portions and wrapped for the freezer, ready for instant use. He must still discover for himself, and display for his audience, not only the nature of the fraud he thinks has been perpetrated but a new way of coming at the rock-bottom truth that will be persuasively better than the stale crusts at hand. He is first obliged to destroy an illusion and then to replace it with something else.

The job of destroying and replacing is going on now, rather violently in some quarters. And some of the violence is due to a fundamental disagreement about the nature of the task, which brings me to the second of the echoes that Salinger stirred in me. The noisiest and quite possibly the most influential response now being made to the challenge of a decayed stock naturalism in the theater is a response very much like Salinger's.

It is the effort to kill off naturalistic illusion by calling mocking attention to how it is made. In Jack Gelber's *The Connection*, which has brought fame and limited fortune to an avant-garde organization known as The Living Theatre, the audience enters the uncurtained playhouse to discover unidentified personnel moving in listless preoccupation about the unready stage. In due time it is directly addressed by a not very articulate representative of the management and awkwardly introduced to a not very confident author. Once the "action" has begun and a variety of dope addicts are making fitful conversation by way of shutting out their pain as they wait for a "fix," a team of documentary film makers appears at the edge of the platform to photograph the proceedings for use at some other time. Between scenes, a home-movie projector flashes onto a wrinkled curtain a jumbled stream of rehearsal shots in which the same actors who are now made up and costumed are seen at their ease and in mufti.

The play is not real, it is written; we have met the author,

and he is still lurking about somewhere. The action is not a continuity, not an unfolding narrative; it is subject to interruption at any time by photographers who are recording it in fragments which may, or may not, be put together later. The characters are not people, they remain actors: if we are not convinced of this as one of them circulates among us in the lobby at intermission time, we will have it rammed home every time the projector lights up to show us the players when they were only playing at playing.

This is not precisely the same thing as Bertolt Brecht's celebrated doctrine of "alienation," but it is related to it. "It must at all times be made apparent to the spectators," writes Martin Esslin in his recent study of the German writer-director, "that they are not witnessing real events happening before their very eyes at *this very moment*," but are sitting in a theater where "the director must strive to produce by all the means at his disposal effects that will keep the audience separate, estranged, alienated from the action."

Nor is it necessarily and in all respects the identical atmosphere director Joan Littlewood and author Brendan Behan have so lustily established in their jig-play *The Hostage*. (*The Hostage* begins with the entire company lined up at the footlights, dancing a jig in cheerful defiance of the somber plot and in open contempt of the realistic setting, dancing simply so that we shall like them and feel livened up; the evening ends on the same note.) But again the similarities are unmistakable. Should the story show signs of moving forward, it must instantly be aborted by an irrelevant song; an actor drops, or elides, his characterization in order to tell us, confidentially, that he is going to sing the song; the song itself is not content with being irrelevant, it must also outrage us (there's one, accompanied by a dainty shuffle around an invisible Maypole, called "We're Here Because We're Queer"). The hero is killed by rifle shots near curtain time; he rises to join his friends in the final song.

Each of these violations of our most familiar model has a somewhat different end in view. *The Connection* seems to me to be knifing the naturalistic illusion in order to become more, not less, naturalistic; the shock to our ordinary theatrical expectations is quickly followed by realities so shocking —the squeezing of pus from a boil, the insertion of a needle into an addict's arm—that they would probably not have been tolerable in a politely organized exhibit. (The very notion of selective organization would most likely have excluded them.) Brecht wished to alienate his audience in order to educate it; if he could persuade people that what was happening was not true inside the playhouse but was true *outside* it, he would have made them better socialists, or better Communists, or just plain better thinkers. *The Hostage* seems the disruptive ebullience of a man rather than a theory, an explosion of personality that means to be personal and in no way confined, a case of Brendan Behan going to his own head.

But they do have in common an iconoclastic determina-

The play that represents the current extreme of anti-form theater in New York is Jackson MacLow's The Marrying Maiden. *In it the actions of the players are determined not by a text but by throws of dice during the performance, each resulting number standing for one of several set responses; thus the pandemonic activity shown in this picture occurs at a different time each evening.*

tion to knock naturalistic form as we know it square on the noggin. They are sometimes despairing and sometimes merry as they go about their work, and they may find themselves, when this first work is done, driving at last in assorted directions. For the moment, however, they share an eagerness to call into question the fundamental assumption on which our earlier drama rested, the assumption that we were to "suspend disbelief" when the curtain went up, that we were to try hard not to notice the part that canvas and grease paint and long hours of rehearsing and rewriting might have played in all this. We are now asked to *notice*, to disbelieve, to stop short abruptly when we have begun to accept too much. The house is being taken apart for us; each of its supporting members is being held up to scorn in its impotent isolation; later on, perhaps, we shall put the pieces together in some other way.

And then again, perhaps we won't. There are indications that some of our doubters are not simply wrecking the house in order to rebuild it. Some, it would seem, are thinking of taking a still deeper plunge. It is possible to go beyond the dismantling of a shabby framework that was only regarded as being temporary anyway toward a profound distrust of all framework as such. It is possible, that is, not only to recoil from one tired shape that art has taken during a certain time in history, but to recoil, absolutely, from art.

Suppose, some of our writers seem to be saying, all art automatically falsifies? The merest gesture toward shapeliness, the tiniest tuck here or there in the fabric borrowed from life, the very orderliness of a progressive narrative or of a consciously tooled sentence—all, all are cheats. The moment you touch what *is* with the wand of style, the moment you arrange either words or events in such a way that the arrangement itself becomes attractive, a fraud has been perpetrated. Truth has been turned into artifice, and the archi-

tectural outcome whatever its shape cannot help being a lie.

The fear that every effort toward conscious art may prove a liability—a prettifying fig leaf upon the naked truth or an arbitrary barrier between the artist and the actual impulse that roils within him—is with us, above and beyond the simple desire to wash away one tired formula. *The Connection* does not rest its case on occasional interruptions, is not content with reminding us that a playwright is loose in the auditorium. It wants also to insist that the playwright, that deliberate artificer, is a plain excrescence, however present he may be.

The playwright, we are told, may have initiated something —the idea for the evening, the first tick of the clock in a particular place, perhaps. But he has not been permitted to design its movement thereafter. The actors, given the playwright's first push, have been commanded to "improvise." They are not improvising, of course; Mr. Gelber has written down the things they are supposed to be making up, and we have subtly returned to the theater of illusion even while we are loudly denying its existence. But the denial is there. The pretense that there is to be no pretense is there. "That's the way it is, man," sighs a voice at the back of the meeting-house, encouraging us to accept the proceedings as a factual record, a bit of spontaneous combustion, that has never been tampered with or even mildly encouraged. We are urged to believe that what we are watching is as free to be itself as the hand of the action painter, attacking a canvas before thought has spoiled its pure energy.

A subsequent bill at The Living Theatre has attempted to remove the air of lingering falsification that clings to *The Connection*. Even the pretense to no pretense must go. In Jackson MacLow's *The Marrying Maiden*, part of a bill called *The Theatre of Chance*, the playwright proclaims that he has *not* written down the sequence. He has left it to the

45

throw of the dice. Numbers are rolled at random by a master stage manager, and the actors must swing into movement not according to the dictates of a prepared text that can be read but under the immediate impact of mathematical whim. The theory, if I understand it correctly (the program notes do not make this altogether easy), is that the director has staged a certain number of ready responses which can be summoned forth by the players as the triggering numbers are called. The shape that any one evening may take can therefore never be premeditated; we are present not at something determined but at something still in the process of being "done." Calculation kills, and we must turn to chance to feel the warmth of the creative spark.

Chance is not Salinger's method; he seems to be aiming instead at total candor, at an unburdening that will relieve him not only of his memories of the brother he is writing about (the controlled selectivity of art would suppress some of these memories and so tell a lie of omission) but also of the charge of having created a character who, coming to exist in his own right, will acquire an independent identity (and so constitute a lie of commission).

But whatever technical methods are marshaled to meet it, the fear of the lie is the bogey that confronts us; it accounts, I think, for two quotations that Mr. Salinger has called to the colors at the beginning of his non-story, his anti-story. From Kafka he summons the thought that "the actors by their presence always convince me, to my horror, that most of what I've written about them until now is false," in spite of the fact that it has been written "with steadfast love." (An immediate parenthesis adds that "even now, while I write it down, this, too, becomes false.") Deception creeps in between the muscle and the scrawl.

And from Kierkegaard he has taken the figurative notion that the management of art is like a slip of life's pen. Such a small clerical error may perhaps be "no error but in a far higher sense . . . an essential part of the whole exposition." Still, it is a fib, and a fib that forbids the author to correct it, as though it were saying in Kierkegaard's words, "No, I will not be erased, I will stand as a witness against thee, that thou art a very poor writer." Something essential to art may make a dishonest man of the artist. For some years to come we may find a good many desperately serious men making public confession of such sins.

But there is a third and last echo to be accounted for here, and its sound has not the least trace of *mea culpa* in it. Moving directly against the almost maddened urge to kill all artifice is a fresh and cunning determination, on the part of certain sorcerers, to break with our weary formula and to get more "truth" into the work by doubling, tripling, and quadrupling the amount of artifice. More, not less, is the battle cry here.

If this seems an odd plan of campaign, a quick glance at Jean Anouilh's *The Waltz of the Toreadors* may serve as an intelligible map. Anouilh is every bit as fed up as his adventurous contemporaries with the familiar theater of apparent fact; I do not know that he has ever written a play that could properly be called realistic. He is also eager to explore a specifically contemporary content, to dig more deeply into our romantic despairs and our hard-headed idiocies than a conventional form, with its careful comings and goings and time wasted on cocktails, would permit him to do.

But his method of dismissing the torpid and limiting theater of naturalistic illusion is to substitute for it an alienated form that is even more formal than the old one. Instead of shooting for the declared formlessness of *The Connection,* he imports and imposes upon himself the severely stylized, rigidly run, absurdly polished machinery of mistaken-identity farce. *The Waltz of the Toreadors* is set inside a burnished glass showcase borrowed from a Victorian aunt: the characters flirt at glossy cross purposes, aborted twin suicides take place at the same comic moment, the rival in the living room is the old romantic's long-lost son. The façade is pure nonsense, erected according to unalterable laws.

We are delightedly aware that it is nonsense; and our awareness kills off, and gleefully mocks, the plausible theater we are tired of just as certainly as the "alienation" theater does. This is, we know, unreal—a preposterous conceit. It is also a frame. It is, on the one hand, an easy frame of reference: we recognize at once the artifice we are dealing with, we have our bearings, we know what moves to expect and how the farce will work out. On the other hand, it is a frame that, being so swiftly recognized *as a frame,* can be taken for granted and, in effect, dismissed. Because we know so well every foolishly overdressed nook and cranny of the silly house we have been invited to, we are free to give our full attention to what may be going on inside it.

Anouilh has been freed by the same stroke: having to give no more than impish lip service to a predictable style, to a cheerfully prefabricated outline, he can fill the great empty space inside it with anything he likes. What he does do, now, is fill the bonbon box with sad and angry and wistful and wicked human emotions, all the more harrowing at heart for the strict and mindless gaiety of the surface. Anouilh's box is not at all like the plausible "box" Thornton Wilder rebelled against but is as gracefully decorated as Pandora's; it has also been opened.

The discovery of a new reality inside a deliberate archaism is not a trick to be confined to comedy, if *The Waltz of the Toreadors* can really be called a comedy. Young Jack Richardson, with *The Prodigal,* suggested that the trappings of the Oresteia legend—narrative and even costumes intact—constitute a pattern that is at once familiar and unreal, inside which vigorous new comment can be made. One rigs up the tent for circus or for battle; an area has now been circumscribed, artificially, and its arbitrariness may still be mocked as Cassandra mocks it in *The Prodigal,* but it has become a shelter in which pressing and perceptive fresh work may get done. "To know the future means knowing what men will do," Cassandra says, but "what they feel while doing it is quite another matter."

Nor do all of those who are choosing to work inside a set of firm, even foolish, regulations feel themselves bound to adopt a regulatory pattern belonging to one or another time in the past. In the theater the Swiss iconoclast Friedrich Duerrenmatt has sometimes thrown his weight on the side of anti-form: in such a play as *Fools Are Passing Through* he causes his nightmare characters to ring down lecture charts from the heavens in order to make sure that we are not lured into the illusion of continuing, believably imitated life. He has sometimes shifted footing and used the stylized conceits of mythological farce: *The Jackass* puts on an ancient mask and keeps it there. But as we move with him to the other end of the bookstore and dip into his most characteristic novels, we find him beguiling us by seeming to observe the rules of a quite rigid, and wholly contemporary, genre. He uses the most conventional and commonplace of twentieth-century formulas, that of the detective story, to map out his terrain.

There is a nasty murder somewhere in Switzerland. There is an aging detective, bitterly determined to ferret out the culprit. There is an investigation, there are many false leads, there is the thrill of a chase. And there is, as well, a solution to the mystery—in *The Pledge* and again in *The Judge and the Hangman*. We are given a promise of form, we move for a very long while in the well-oiled grooves of a form, we are never absolutely denied the pleasures of that form. But the helpful shape contains a secret: Mr. Duerrenmatt has made a convenience of the convention (a convention has no other purpose than to be a convenience) and has performed its ancient and arbitrary gestures only to bring us the quicker toward an unexpected aberration, a shocking psychological insight, a snatch of highly personal philosophy. The silverware is what we are accustomed to; the meat it is used to cut is something else again.

Those who are straining mightily to keep artifice alive as a kind of mutually understood chessboard on which new games can be played are faced with sobering problems. They are severely dependent upon borrowed frames from the past or upon frames from the present that are, like Duerrenmatt's detective-story gambit, so completely stylized as to constitute a rigging that cannot be mistaken for the naturalistic illusionism we are forced to abandon. Their problem is to arrive at a fresh style that will be seen and accepted *as a style*, much as Restoration comedy must have been blithely and knowingly accepted by British gentlemen of the seventeenth century or as a performance by the Kabuki is still accepted by gentlemen of Japan. You will often find their partisans studying the calculated unrealities of the Kabuki or of the Piccolo Teatro di Milano playing Goldoni's *Servant of Two Masters*, wondering how so deliberate an artificing can be indigenously arrived at for the twentieth century.

Those who are heaving their shoulders in the contrary di-

In The Good Woman of Setzuan *Bertolt Brecht succeeded in removing the illusion of naturalism from the stage by the use of charades and other stylized forms of performance which comment on life without imitating it.*

rection have their problems, too. One problem, really. Forms can be destroyed by mockery. Form itself can be destroyed by inserting a quick cancellation of its virtues each time one or another virtue threatens to catch hold of an audience. But a dismissal of all artifice, and a distrust of all that is or may become art, at last tends to paralyze. If a "small clerical error" inevitably crops up whenever anything is transcribed from life to page or stage, and if this "essential" error is to be regarded as fatal, dare we ever transcribe anything at all?

I have been trying not to take sides in this partial account of the contest to date, though I am naturally a side-taker and find such virtuous conduct difficult. But we are gradually being confronted with a choice between absolutes, or so it would seem on this clouded spring day at the beginning of the sixties, and the time may come when we feel excited enough to cast votes. The rival positions are becoming reasonably clear. At one end of the fraying rope the anti-form team is crying, "Be honest, never lie!" in terms so uncompromising that every measure of control over the materials of life must be unconditionally surrendered. At the other the formalists are suggesting, with a faint smile and a shrug, "Lie, but lie in such a way that the lie is obvious and in no way deceiving; the scaffold of the honest lie will give you something to walk on, somewhere to go."

Walter Kerr, a frequent contributor to Horizon, *is drama critic of the New York* Herald Tribune. *He is writing a new book about America, to be titled* The Decline of Pleasure.

THE KNIGHTS OF THE MALTESE CROSS

Founded to care for the sick in the Holy Land, the Order

of St. John became the military arm of the Crusader state.

Eight centuries later it still carries on its rescue work

By EDITH SIMON

In the time of the Crusades a new type of religious sprang up, that of the fighting monk or clerical knight—whichever designation one prefers; for both were contradictions in terms, reconciled by the medieval genius for applied casuistry. The two leading bodies of these Military Orders, as they were called, were the Templars and the Hospitallers— the Poor Fellow-Soldiers of Christ and the Temple of Solomon, and the Knights of St. John's Hospital at Jerusalem. Formed under very similar auspices and playing, indeed, identical roles during the two centuries of holy war in Palestine, they became utterly divergent in their ultimate fate.

The Templars perished miserably, with a bang reverberating through the nations. The Knights of St. John quietly metamorphosed themselves time and again and thrive to this day. Thousands benefit year in, year out from the many philanthropic institutions, medical and otherwise, under the sign of the octagonal cross. But how many of them realize that the emblem belongs to an extraterritorial sovereign power with recognized diplomatic envoys to the governments of many nations, with the right to issue valid passports and confer honors and decorations, and—final proof of being indeed a state—possessing an air fleet of its own? How many are aware that modern ambulance organizations descend directly from the Military Knights of Outremer?

Outremer—Overseas, and specifically the Holy Land—had been the goal of European pilgrims throughout the Middle Ages. Several decades before the launching of the First Crusade a group of merchants of Amalfi decided to endow a

*In the Great Hall at Rhodes the fortieth Grand Master of the Order, Pierre d'Aubusson, sits in state among his Knights.
He was the hero of the first siege of Rhodes in 1480, when the Knights beat off a sea-borne Turkish force of 70,000 men.
To commemorate the victory Guillaume Caoursin, a vice-chancellor of the Order, wrote an eyewitness account and had it
illustrated in Rhodes. In this frontispiece of the manuscript Caoursin is shown presenting his book to the Grand Master.*

il aloit vestu tout seulement et en la matinee
estoit froide comme dit vous ay il ot vestu
une pellice debrebis toute enuerse et bien
ressembloit derbis. Et lempereur son vient
dehors sa tente et sachiez quil auoit labeue
non mie bien clere ainz voit et apperceuoit
moult petit en especial chose qui feust au
quel somit si regarda vers la grant place
qui deuant son logeiz estoit et vit la maur
de ses barons assemblez et ne sauoit lacuise

lors apperceust pluseur de ses barons a
une part qui conseilloient et auec eu
vit Galeaz et lui suaduiz pour lapelte
ce que ce feust un lyon. Lors lempereur
dist. ha las ie voy mains de mes barō
aconseil qui ne maiment mie trop ne
obeissent et voy en leur compaignie
un lyon par semblant moult prise de
eulx ie ai grant doubte ay quils ne se mer
tent de vour amor. car iay vestu ceste

hospice for Christian pilgrims at Jerusalem; with the Caliph's consent, the whole country then being under Moslem rule, they dedicated the foundation to St. John the Almsgiver.

The First Crusade, a huge straggling international pilgrimage of Christian warriors with the aim of wresting the Holy Places from the Moslem (to whom these were variously holy, too), was launched in 1096. The Crusader armies, what remained of them after over three years' catastrophic detours, clashes, and privations, laid siege to Jerusalem on arrival there in June, 1099, and on July 15 broke victoriously into the city. Fearful massacre ensued, in which many native Christians were erroneously slain because, like the Moslem citizens, they had beards. Others, more easily identified because they were found in Moslem prisons, fared better; and among those victims of Moslem reprisal was the Blessed Gerard, Rector of St. John's Hospital. He immediately resumed his duties and with great vigor sought to meet the enormously increased demands upon the Hospital following the siege and attendant on the consolidation of the Christian conquests in what came to be called the Latin Kingdom.

The Hospital had at first been run by Benedictine monks. But with Gerard in command, charge of it passed entirely to a group of knights who, in recoil from a surfeit of bloodshed, had been attracted to the charity and who offered it, in addition to humbler services, their armed protection. They formed themselves into a monastic Brotherhood and took the three vows of poverty, chastity, and obedience before the Patriarch of Jerusalem in the Church of the Holy Sepulchre.

The Papal Bull of 1113, confirming the Hospitallers' status as an Order and granting them various privileges and exemptions as well as the right to adopt uniform habit, created one far-reaching though then seemingly incidental change. Henceforth the Knights of St. John were no longer the particular liege men of the Patriarch of Jerusalem, the local head of the Christian Church, but were sworn exclusively to the sovereign authority of the pope. The importance of this change became more apparent as presently the Order added specific, positive military functions to its humanitarian ones.

Herein the Knights of St. John followed the example of the Knights of the Temple of Solomon, who banded together in 1118 along much the same lines, with the difference that in the activities of the latter the emphasis from the first lay expressly on armed combat. The Templars' prime aim was to protect the roads of the Crusader commonwealth and ensure the safety of unceasing streams of pilgrims. Since even at the height of its prosperity the Commonwealth consisted of scattered territories linked tenuously enough by a system of strategically placed castles and watchtowers, since what bore the name of road was seldom more than wilderness modified somewhat, and since enemy marauders lay everywhere in wait, effective police activity was badly needed.

The Templars, like the Hospitallers, started out in allegiance to the Patriarchate of Jerusalem, like them were soon after relieved of acknowledging any authority save the pope's, and like them enjoyed a steady growth of enthusiastic support among all classes and in every country of the Christian world. Enthusiasm and support were manifested not only in a wildfire increase of membership but also by donations ranging from small sums and simple household articles to very large gifts of land and valuable revenues from the kings and great nobles of Europe, as well as privileges and exemptions, both ecclesiastical and temporal, spelling perpetual enhancement of wealth and of power. Accordingly, the Knights of the Hospital exchanged St. John the Almsgiver for a more prominent saint, St. John the Baptist, when the scope, influence, and renown of the House appeared to have outgrown its original patron.

The two Military Orders by degrees became rivals. In Europe as in Palestine they competed for recruits, for the gifts of the faithful, and for political supremacy, no less than for honor of arms, generosity towards the poor, and primogeniture. For centuries they quarreled as to which Order was truly the first—the Hospitallers having as it were invented the whole basic idea, the Templars claiming the credit for that extraordinary synthesis, the *fighting* monk. A time came when they fought it out in pitched battles; indeed there was a period when the two Orders were formally at war.

In one respect, however, they remained united: at feud with the Patriarchate. For as the Patriarchate stood in perennial conflict with both the Crown of Jerusalem and the Holy

THE LEADERS OF THE CRUSADES

This illustration from a fourteenth-century French epic depicts a purely fanciful gathering of the Crusader chieftains. Crests on the tents bear the lions of England and the crossed keys of the Papacy. The figure with the triple crown is surely a pope, and the ecclesiastic in the golden robe, talking to a cardinal, may be the Patriarch of Jerusalem. The king in red might be Richard the Lion-Hearted. The bearded figure wearing a black robe with Maltese cross could hardly be other than the leader of the Hospital—either the Blessed Gerard, its founder, or Raymond du Puy, who succeeded him as Grand Master in 1120. The medieval French text is part of a rambling epic poem, a roman de chevalerie, *written by Thomas de Saluces.*

See in Rome, the Military Orders, which had meanwhile emerged as the hard core of the Crown's otherwise fluctuating armies, were thus doubly involved. Temple and Hospital might advocate completely opposed policies, they might back different candidatures to the throne—but in causing even petty irritation to the Patriarch they were ever at one. Where the Templars contented themselves with the simple amusement of shooting arrows at the door of the Church of the Holy Sepulchre, the most sacred sanctuary known to Christendom, "to disturb the congregation" while the Patriarch celebrated mass, the Hospitallers went so far as to build tall towers facing that church, whence they would ring great bells to drown the Patriarch's voice when he wished to address the people.

That they could do this with impunity is a measure of the power attained by the Military Orders. Soon no king could be crowned at Jerusalem without the consent of both Grand Masters. No treaty was considered valid by the enemy unless it bore the seals of the Temple and St. John's Hospital. Autonomous bodies within the State, outside the royal jurisdiction neither Order would hold itself bound by any agreement lacking such ratification. In a lesser degree the same applied outside the Holy Land, in the Crusaders' European mother countries; everywhere, by virtue of their vast holdings and immunities, the commanderies of the Military Orders formed such sovereign enclaves. And incidentally, potentially, the Military Orders—a standing, well-trained fighting force, in fact the only disciplined army in the world—might serve as an instrument at the unique disposal of the Papacy. They thus excited distrust, envy, calumny, and fear, besides individual gratitude and universal admiration.

At the Vatican the rivalry between the two principal strains of "Christ's Militia" was regarded in the light of salutary competition; and among the Latin colonists disunity was no reproach, seeing that disunity was the chief ingredient of the whole Kingdom's political climate. Disunity, in the long run, was to prove the ruin of Outremer; the first campaign in which the Hospitallers marched as Military Knights under their own banner was King Baldwin II's punitive expedition of 1131 against his own daughter, the rebellious princess of Antioch

—that is, against fellow Christians and not against the Infidel.

It is always easy to be cynical, and always tempting, if only because the discreditable anecdote will tend to be more entertaining than accounts of virtue and integrity. The temptation is all the greater when one deals with the Crusading period, which in the teeth of some two centuries of serious historical scholarship continues enwrapped in the tenacious tissues of a false romanticism. It is not so easy to remember that the complexities of practical life inevitably make havoc of the tidy theoretical principle, and to balance shortcomings with achievement.

Pledged to poverty, the Military Knights amassed fabulous riches and became the chief landowners and builders of castles in the Holy Land; pledged to humility, their arrogance became proverbial; pledged to make war on the enemies of the Faith, they took turns in concluding alliances with the notorious Moslem sect of the Assassins, whose avocation of political homicide has made their name a lasting synonym for "murderer." Pledged to serve "our lords the sick," St. John's Hospital at Jerusalem in course of time reversed the diet originally prescribed of white bread and wine for its charges, coarse rations and water for the Brethren.

But withal the Knights of St. John did feed, house, and tend between one and two thousand sick people daily, at Jerusalem alone—not counting their other hospices all over the country and their rest houses for pilgrims on their way across Europe, and not to mention pensioners. Unlike the Templars, who eventually asked the Western secular authorities to restrain from pilgrimage the aged and infirm and the poor, since "such folk only became a burden on the Military Orders overseas," the Knights of St. John never lost sight of their fundamental purpose. Without the means to maintain a wide-flung international organization they could scarcely have discharged their pious task to the tune of such numbers so comprehensively. They shared with the Templars the brunt of defending the isolated frontier outposts of the realm, of which Krak des Chevaliers—at least twice the size of the largest fortresses in medieval France—remains so splendid and impressive an example. Splendid and impressive, too, were their courage and striking power in war and their fortitude in captiv-

TEXT CONTINUED ON PAGE 56

KNIGHTLY NOMENCLATURE

THE MEMBERS OF

THE ORDER OF THE HOSPITAL OF ST. JOHN OF JERUSALEM

COMMONLY CALLED

THE KNIGHTS OF ST. JOHN

OR

THE HOSPITALLERS

WERE LATER KNOWN AS

THE KNIGHTS OF RHODES

AND LATER STILL AS

THE KNIGHTS OF MALTA

THE CAPTURE OF JERUSALEM

The goal and climax of the First Crusade was the siege of Jerusalem in the summer of 1099. Though painted four centuries later for a history by Sebastien Mamerot, this miniature, with its milling troops, prancing mounts, and strolling ladies, is not wholly unfaithful to that highly disorganized military operation. Failing to take the city by escalade, the Crusaders, under Godefroy de Bouillon, built heavy towers, rolled them up to the walls, and from these were able to take the city. From a Moslem jail they freed the founder of the Order of the Hospital, the Blessed Gerard.

KRAK OF THE KNIGHTS

At the vulnerable waist of the Latin Kingdom, guarding the sole pass to Tripoli from the Moslem hinterland, the Crusaders set the greatest of their castles, Krak of the Knights. Clamped on a spur of the foothills, its vast yet shapely bulk has survived eight hundred years with remarkably little change. . . . The salient feature of the fortress is its strictly concentric plan. The walls of the outer ward are at every point dominated by those of the inner. The latter, situated on higher ground, could be held when the outer ward had fallen. Forming the south side of the inner ward is a massive redoubt incorporating three linked towers—a type of arrangement that was replacing the early twelfth-century keeps. This redoubt constituted a third line of defense tenable when even the inner ward had fallen. The main gate and its supplementary defenses are admirably contrived. To penetrate the inner castle, a besieging force had to thrust its way up a vaulted passage having three elbow-turns—a device much favored by the Saracens—and defended by an external moat, a drawbridge, four gates, and at least one portcullis, the last a Frankish innovation in the Holy Land.

The defense along the curtain walls is beautifully devised. A series of round towers—the latter towards the end of the twelfth century began to replace the more vulnerable square tower—spaced at short intervals provide complete covering fire . . . the inner ward is provided with a gigantic talus as a protection against mining, and the wide ditch, characteristic of Byzantine fortification, has been transformed into a moat so large as to resemble a small lake. A number of posterns made sortie easy. They were so placed that a party fighting its way back to safety presented their shield-side to the enemy. A windmill on the ramparts ground corn for the garrison, and the storage chambers were immense. At the castle of Margat, not far to the north, we are told that similar chambers held provision for a thousand men for a five-year siege. Famine was not a weapon that could easily be used against the defenders of Krak.

The history of the castle is only less remarkable than its fortifications. Lying upon the borders of the Kingdom, it was the regular meeting place for expeditions launched into the Moslem hinterland. Conversely, as the gateway to Tripoli and the coast, it was the first Frankish defense against which repeated Saracen attacks were delivered. . . .

It was only after the middle of the thirteenth century, when the final and fatal decadence of the Franks had set in, that Krak began to experience serious difficulties. . . . In 1271 [the Sultan] Beibars, with his ally the Grand Master of the Assassins, and a large army, invested the castle. The Hospitallers who constituted the strength of the garrison were experienced soldiers, and as the Saracens admitted, fought with tenacity; but they were hopelessly outnumbered. The large perimeter of the outer ward was soon abandoned. Even so it was a month before one of the towers of the inner ward fell to the Moslems. The surviving Knights then withdrew to the great redoubt. . . . At all events he [Beibars] preferred ruse to attack. A forged letter is said to have been smuggled into the redoubt, purporting to come from the Frankish commander at Tripoli, and ordering the Hospitallers to surrender. They did so under promise of safe-conduct to the coast. and on April 8th, 1271, Krak capitulated. It had been in Crusader hands for a hundred and sixty-one years.

Robin Fedden in *History Today*

TEXT CONTINUED FROM PAGE 52

ity. After the disastrous Sixth and Seventh Crusades they were almost exterminated, yet contrived to replenish themselves and rise again, till in effect the Military Orders were left the only stable element of the Latin Kingdom.

There is a pretty legend that the Christians' great opponent, Saladin, desiring to find out whether the fame of the Knights of St. John rested on truth, entered the Hospital at Jerusalem in the disguise of a poor pilgrim. Received according to the Rule, which laid down that "each sick person was to be treated as if he were the Master of the House," the false pilgrim refused all food that was offered him and when pressed said at last that there was only one dish he would be able to eat: a broth made from the feet of Morel, the horse of the Grand Master. So the Grand Master, "death in his soul," had his cherished horse led forth for the sacrifice—whereupon Saladin revealed himself, stayed the slaughter, and departed with many expressions of admiration.

The story is a nice example of representative truth, in regard to both the charity of the Hospital and the chivalry of Saladin. It seems almost churlish to append the factual truth that upon the reconquest of Jerusalem by Saladin, the former Hospital area was given the name of Muristan, or madhouse —though the tradition that this witty notion was the Sultan's own does not appear to be attested.

So little is known about the Blessed Gerard that even his birthplace and family name are in dispute; but contemporary praises of his character are so warm as to suggest rather more than the stereotype obituary. He evidently gave himself up to the practical task in hand, which left him little time for the theological or even the wider administrative implications of the enterprise he had set going. Under him no special statutes were drawn up, the Knights of St. John living roughly under a modified version of the Augustinian code. It was under Gerard's successor, Raymond du Puy, that the military function of the Order was evolved and its own Rule and ceremonial were laid down.

The Brethren were divided into three classes—Knights, Serving Brothers, and Chaplains—to which became added Associate Knights, and Sisters to look after the women pilgrims. As with the Templars, the candidate for professed knighthood had first of all to prove that he was of noble descent on both sides before taking his vows and stripping himself of all private possessions and worldly ties. But over and above the stress on the care of the sick, there were two other significant differences between the respective Rules of the two Orders—significant more in view of later developments than at the time of publication.

The Templars early evinced the obsession with security of the predominantly military mind; and secrecy, extending gradually to all their internal transactions whatsoever, became positively sacrosanct with them. Infringements of their law of secrecy were punished more severely almost than any other misdemeanor; and the mystery with which the Order came rather to plume itself lent plentiful fuel to rumors of

TEXT CONTINUED ON PAGE 60

56

ᚦHE SIEGE OF RHODES

With the fall of Constantinople in 1453, the Knights' citadel at Rhodes became the eastern outpost of Christian power in the Mediterranean. Its fortification was the work of Grand Master Pierre d'Aubusson, who took office in 1476 and had but four years to transform it into a bristling citadel, shown at right, before the Turkish assault began. This bird's-eye view and the two scenes which follow are taken from the same eyewitness history whose frontispiece appears on page 50. The year is 1480; the Turkish fleet of a hundred and sixty ships is anchored at top right, while Turkish troops surround the fortress walls. At bottom center is the main harbor, guarded by the two towers of St. Michael and St. John, built upon the rocky bases which probably once supported the legs of the Colossus. At bottom right is St. Nicholas Tower, the strongest but also the most vulnerable because of the shallow water surrounding it. Twice the Turkish vizier launched his galleys against St. Nicholas Tower; twice, from the land, he besieged the Jewish Quarter at the lower left corner of the citadel. At the height of the battle the Knights were rallied by the sight of the Grand Master fighting on the walls in golden armor and finally, at the crisis, by a vision of St. John and the Virgin in the sky overhead. Disheartened by the loss of nine thousand men in one day and by a rumor of reinforcements for the Knights, the Turks departed, not to return again until forty-two years later when, after almost six months of siege, they finally forced the Knights to surrender and leave the island forever.

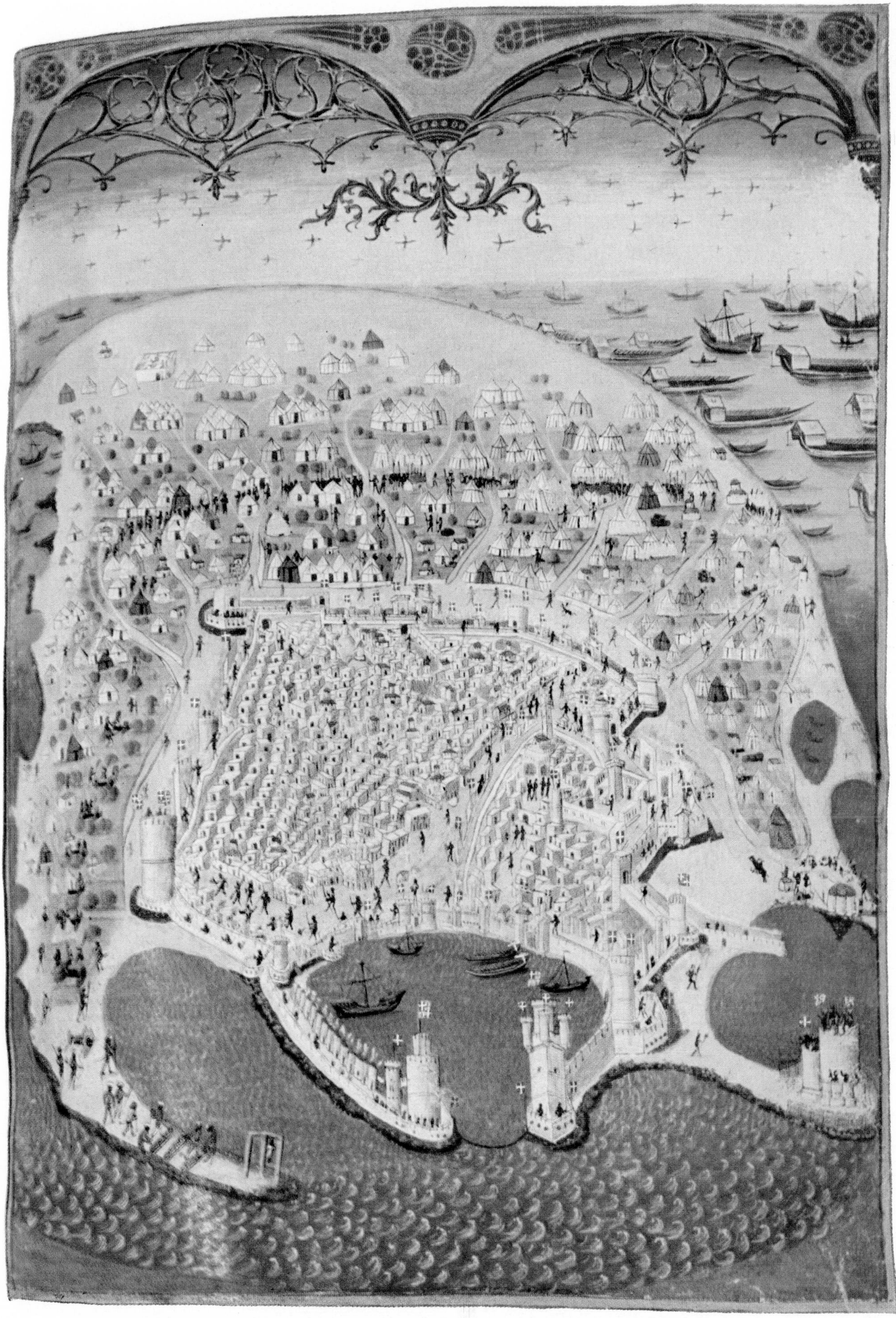

BIBLIOTHEQUE NATIONALE

Turks surround the city walls in this placid scene. An arrow bearing a message has been shot into the fortress, perhaps by a Christian spy in the Turkish camp; a man picks it up and hands it to the Grand Master.

Atop St. Nicholas Tower, tight-packed Knights repel the Turkish galleys. The assault was near success when the wind shifted, allowing the Knights to launch a fleet of fireships. The galleys retreated, leaving the troops to die.

TEXT CONTINUED FROM PAGE 56

dark goings-on behind the locked doors of the Temple—fuel for the pyres on which the Templar Order perished finally.

Although scandal did not spare the Order of St. John—as it will spare no exclusive group nor any community of holy appearance—the lack of secrecy surrounding the proceedings of the Hospital blunted scandal's edge.

The second obsession of the Templars which the Hospitallers did not share was a preoccupation with sexual default, passing well beyond what was to be expected even of a religious society of the time. The Rule of the Temple contained so many stringent provisions against the danger of sodomy and went to such lengths in forbidding even the remotest contact with the female sex, that the Order was almost bound to be accused of those very transgressions it showed so much anxiety to prevent.

To be sure, the Rule of St. John had its regulations concerning fornication; but here the penalties are surprisingly mild. One marvels to read, for instance, that the culprit "if he shall have sinned in secret [shall] repent in secret and impose upon himself a suitable penance"—which seems trusting to the point of laxity. And even if the sin "shall be well known and proved beyond question," a public beating followed by expulsion followed by readmittance was a relatively light, brisk punishment, considering the epoch in all its brooding and brutal fanaticism.

When the Temple at length allowed associate membership to women, this was in breach of statutes that had never been rescinded and therefore yet another of their crimes; whereas within the rival Brotherhood the Sisters working in the special female hospices played a natural and honored part from the beginning. They wore robes of the same color as the undress mantles of the Brethren: black, with the eight-pointed cross of white which figured also on their scarlet battle standard.

Desertion from the gonfalon in battle was reckoned the most serious offense a Military Knight could commit, and expulsion thereupon was final. But such acts were of very rare occurrence. The celebrated gallantry of the fighting monks was not exceptional among men of their class, bred to combat from the cradle; but the disciplined co-ordination which again and again caused the astonished comment that they "fought as one body" was unparalleled at the time. The knight on horseback was equivalent to the armored vehicle of today: to appreciate the value of a constant complement of close to a thousand Knights in Palestine (supported by several times that number of infantry and other retainers), one has to perform the arithmetical feat of multiplying flesh and blood by imaginary steel plating and motor power.

Also, like the Church itself, in corporate existence the Military Orders were constant and imperishable, in contrast to the secular forces of the Latin Kingdom which were in everlasting flux. Any warrior having done whatever crusading stint he had privately vowed to encompass could go home —to be replaced by newcomers without experience of the country and prevailing conditions, from climate to modes of warfare and diplomacy. As time went on and the Christian-held territories began to crumble away, more and more went home and fewer and fewer came. By the early thirteenth century the very Crown of Jerusalem had to be hawked about Europe in order to find candidates.

Among the many reasons for the downfall of Outremer was the archaic feudal organization of the realm, in a strict form no longer practicable and already out of date in the West before ever the Latin colonies were set up in the East. Here the king was still little more than a symbol of fealty, a figurehead and war leader, without any real central power or much actual property. The ever-growing trend towards nationalism and modern monarchy throughout Europe became negatively manifest in the Holy Land, supposedly a supranational realm with a society of international composition: for that society fast disintegrated, homeward, as the Latin Kingdom fell into decline. Even the Military Orders had at times to be admonished by the Holy See that Outremer was their *raison d'être* and should be their chief concern, rather than the consolidation of their interests in the countries of the West.

Nevertheless, for some time before the end it was they who in effect constituted the nation of the Latin Kingdom and they who formed its main rear guard at the last.

Jerusalem had been lost for good in 1244. By 1285, when Jean de Villiers was installed as the twenty-second Grand Master of the Hospital, Christian Outremer was but a handful of unconnected strong points in the midst of a huge Moslem empire. In 1291, Acre, the chief remaining fastness of the Crusaders and their seat of government, fell to the enemy after a siege of five weeks. In the final desperate street fighting Grand Master de Villiers was seriously wounded and, despite his vehement and tearful protests, carried on board one of the few ships available for the evacuation of survivors. Behind them, Acre was razed to the ground, and within a few months nothing remained of the Crusader Kingdom.

The human remnants of a lost cause gathered on the island of Cyprus, where De Villiers, recovering, proceeded to rally what was left of the Order of St. John. The Hospitallers' Order was in slightly better case than that of the Knights Templars. The latter's Grand Master had fallen at Acre and was succeeded by one, elected in haste, whose conduct was not calculated to win him the confidence of his subordinates or the respect of others. More important, the Hospitallers' nursing activities received a fresh impetus; there was more need of them and more sympathy for them.

And though doubtless they would not have thanked anyone who told them so, sympathy was what the Military Orders wanted then. It did not take the Western potentates long to start reasoning that since the Orders had been expelled from the Holy Land, they had lost their reason for existence. Over the centuries the Orders had acquired vast possessions of land and treasure in the countries of Western

Gran Galione Del Gran Maestro dell'Ordine f. S. Giovanni di Malta

THE KNIGHTS ON MALTA

*On the island of Malta, in 1530, the Knights began their third and final
period of military glory, this time as a sea power. Their chosen vessel was
the galley, light, swift, responsive to sail or oar, and drawing but three feet
of water. In these little craft they could fire a volley at a larger Moslem ship,
then close in before the enemy could fire. For more than a century they
ruled and protected the sea routes of the Mediterranean. With their red-
striped sail, gilded masts, and red-tipped oars the Maltese galleys made a
brilliant sight—except when they were painted black in token of reconnais-
sance or piracy. For piracy (against the Infidel, to be sure, but in time of
peace piracy, still) was what filled the Order's treasury and furnished slaves.*

*Sultan Suleiman the Magnificent, the conqueror of Rhodes, resolved in
his old age to wipe out the nest from which these corsairs came. In alliance
with Dragut, the Barbary pirate, the Turkish army landed beyond the
Maltese harbor and attacked the Knights' forts from behind. The doughty
old Grand Master, Jean de la Valette, was ready for them. When the Turks
captured Fort St. Elmo and sent the mutilated bodies of the defenders floating across the bay, the Grand Master cut off the heads of his Turkish prisoners and fired them back by cannon. The timely arrival of three hundred
French Knights, followed by a tardy relief force from the king of Spain,
turned the tide and sent the Turk flying from the central Mediterranean.
Both the siege and the maritime exploits of the Maltese Knights are depicted in murals (see pages 63 and 64) in the Grand Master's Palace at the
capital of Malta, now named, in honor of its illustrious defender, Valletta.*

Europe. Now the rulers of these countries, most of them in continuous financial embarrassment, began to cast covetous eyes on these knightly holdings. Greed and economic straits apart, the autonomous Knights, ensconced within a country without being a part of it, were proving a genuine obstacle to national administration.

While the Templars relied on their wealth and power and the friendship of the Papacy to stay encroachments, the Hospitallers swiftly reorganized. They would continue to protect and succor the Christian traveler—at sea if not on land; for the Mediterranean was swarming with Moslem corsairs. The Hospital had long numbered shipbuilding and naval transport among its activities and took the logical step of turning itself into a sea power.

Now under the leadership of Fulk de Villaret, the Knights of St. John were embarking upon the conquest of Rhodes— destined to become their headquarters for the next two hundred years or so—when in 1306 a papal summons went out to the Grand Masters of Hospital and Temple, to attend their Holy Liege at Poitiers in France for a conference about their future.

More than once in the years since the loss of the Holy Land there had been proposals put forward for an amalgamation of the two Orders under greatly changed political and economic auspices, ostensibly for the more effective prosecution of a future Crusade. Both Orders had opposed such a scheme with every argument at their disposal, and so had the Holy See—until the Holy See came to be occupied by a weak pope (Clement V), under the influence of the French king, and moved to France.

Philip the Fair, the fourth of his name on the French throne, had particular designs upon the Military Orders, particular cause to fear them, and a wish to appropriate their possessions. The Military Orders feared no one on earth; but the valor of Fulk de Villaret did not lack discretion, and he excused himself from attending the conference. The Grand Master of the Temple accepted the invitation and rode across France to the meeting as if in triumphal demonstration of his Order's inviolable might. A few weeks later himself and every single Knight, servitor, and dependent of the Temple in France lay in the prisons of King Philip, awaiting a slow process of judicial murder which culminated in the dissolution of the Templar Order six years hence and death at the stake for many leading members.

The charges, which included sorcery, sodomy, and treason, and which the unpopularity of the Templars rendered widely acceptable, did not touch the Hospital, and to the Hospital the Temple's forfeit estate was nominally transferred. But there was reason to fear that King Philip had not yet finished with the Military Orders, and that the rest of the crowned heads of Europe were pondering the example of his success.

Again the Order of St. John reorganized and reoriented itself. It was now adapted to the prevailing trend, split up into seven *national* "Tongues" with the parent Convent of Rhodes acting merely as a federal focus—and it displayed more caution than eagerness in succeeding to the heritage of the Templar estate.

In this the Knights were wiser than they knew.

Considerable portions of the Templar wealth, in state custody throughout the long years when the Temple's fate was in suspense, had insensibly melted away. In accounting for his share the King of France presented a stiff bill, charging among other things six years' board and lodging for the thousands of Templars in his prisons as well as the cost of faggots for the martyrs' pyres. King Edward II of England had rid himself of sundry urgent debts with the aid of Templar property which the recipients were loath to let go again. The remainder was mostly so depreciated by disorder and neglect as to be more liability than asset to the Hospital.

Years of costly litigation ensued and brought the English Tongue to the verge of bankruptcy. Only the intervention of the Grand Prior of Venice, dispatched from Rhodes as a kind of commercial efficiency expert and duly proving the famous acumen of his native merchant republic, set the Order in England on its feet again.

So in England, as in the other countries of the West, the Hospital weathered the storm of progress. But even apart from the dubious Templar inheritance—which included paying out the subsistence allowances awarded to surviving Templars—the catastrophe that had swept the latter away had not passed without affecting also the Knights of St. John. Their very retrenchments helped to place them on a different footing from that which had obtained in the old days. The Order of St. John had been one of the world's great powers; now it was merely one of many similar associations among which it was foremost in right of antiquity only. (There were the Teutonic Knights, who had switched from the Holy Land to the Baltic; the Orders of Christ, of Our Lady of Tortosa, of St. Thomas and St. Lazarus, each of which pursued certain circumscribed functions.)

True, Rhodes remained the furthermost outpost of Christianity against Islam; and the Knights of St. John took a prominent part in the sporadic expeditions to regain a foothold on Moslem territory—attempts which finally ceased in the fifteenth century. But the Knights were not proof against internal corruption, whether as a by-product of returning prosperity or in consequence of the Great Schism (1378–1417) which rent the Order in two just as it did all the rest of Christendom. In their capacity of maritime police, too, the Knights yielded to temptation and somewhat exceeded their sacred duty in the pursuit of unholy piracy.

It was their most ancient purpose, their unforgotten primary allegiance, which upheld continuity of integrity, then as before and in the future. Every evening in the Great Hall of Rhodes *la prière des malades* was solemnly recited with its repetitive address of, *"Seigneurs malades,"* and the explicit reminder that peace on earth and salvation in the next world were the true ends of all Christian striving.

"The Siege of the Battery of St. Elmo, May 27, 1565": In this mural Turkish forces have invested the Knights' two strongholds, Fort St. Angelo at the tip of the peninsula and Fort St. Elmo across the bay, at right. The figures in the fore-ground are probably the Turkish commanders and their ally, Dragut the pirate. Fort St. Elmo fell to the Turks, but Fort St. Angelo stood until it was saved in the scene depicted below: "Arrival of the Great Relief Force, September 17, 1565."

"Entry into Malta of the Venerable General Ruffo, Prior of the Bath, with two Turkish galleys and four prizes, September 23, 1661": Almost a century after the siege the Maltese fleet was still a power in the Mediterranean. Depicted below is another naval exploit in which Maltese galleys captured a much larger Turkish warship. The scene is titled: "Capture of an Algerian vessel in the channel of Malta by the Venerable General Ruffo, Prior of the Bath, January 25, 1661."

For the time being the requirements of this world were observed until the fortifications of Rhodes became the strongest then existing, with due regard to architectonic beauties also, and art treasures began to balance the hoard of bullion and plate in the vaults.

The Ottoman Turks had been in process of becoming the chief power of Islam, and in the early summer of 1480 opened siege on the island, with the aid of 160 ships and 70,000 men, against the Hospital's muster of 450 regular Knights and 4,000 mercenaries. Yet the phrase about the biggest battalions does not necessarily refer to the most numerous, and after nearly three months of incessant bombardment, savage fighting, and appalling losses, it was the Turks who finally withdrew disheartened.

It took another forty-two years before they renewed the assault with an expeditionary force twice as large as the first. Again, in battle the outnumbered Knights more than held their own: the second siege of Rhodes is counted one of the most magnificent episodes in the annals of warfare. But it was not decided by valor and battery. After a few weeks the Ottoman high command desisted from further attempts to take Rhodes by storm and concentrated on blockade, so successfully that after almost six months' heroic resistance the Order of St. John surrendered.

We have to add that the devastating success of the Moslem blockade received assistance at the hands of the Christian powers, too engrossed at that juncture in their own affairs to make very serious efforts to fulfill their obligations towards the Order. After the event all Europe was loud in praises of the glorious defeat: "Nothing in the world was ever lost so splendidly as Rhodes," exclaimed the Emperor Charles V, and salved his conscience by offering the Knights a new home on Malta, granting them full sovereignty against only the homage of one falcon to be sent each year.

On Malta they remained for two hundred and fifty-eight years; and "The Sovereign Order of Malta" became their official title, the octagonal cross henceforth known as the "Maltese." The West still had its bastion against Islam.

However, religious strife and upheaval were not confined to the Levant, and the Order willy-nilly played its part in many a conflict less clear-cut, particularly in England during the fourteenth, fifteenth, and sixteenth centuries.

The Black Death which depleted the populations of Europe about the middle of the fourteenth century had caused a veritable revolution of social conditions in England, which went unrecognized by the legislators. In brief, where previously serfs had abounded, there was now a laborer's market. Peasants and artisans, technically still bound to the soil, cut adrift and lent their services to the highest bidder; and, keeping pace with the increase in the cost of living, wages soared. To put a stop to this, and failing to appreciate an inexorable progression of cause and effect, the government passed the Statute of Laborers, which fixed all wages at their pre-plague level, and followed this up with the Poll Tax, a measure creating fresh hardships and making popular resistance at last inevitable.

In face of the gathering unrest the Treasurer of the Realm resigned, and Robert Hales, Grand Prior of the Hospital in England, took on the onerous vacancy. When, therefore, the revolt broke out in earnest, one of the first places to be sacked and burned by the rebels in London was the Priory of St. John at Clerkenwell. Hales was beheaded on Tower Hill together with the Archbishop of Canterbury, who as Chancellor of the Realm was held responsible for the government. Their heads were stuck on pikes, paraded through the city, and impaled over the gateway of London Bridge.

The rebellion was short-lived, and it was put down with sufficient effect to give feudalism a few hundred years more of grace. But Robert Hales did not remain the only Hospitaller in England to accept the Treasurer's post and die on the block. During the Wars of the Roses, John Langstrother, another Grand Prior, suffered the same fate. And at the time of Henry VIII's conflict with Rome, a number of Knights of St. John also met their end by execution—although in their case the political cause merged once again entirely with the religious, and they died for Faith and conscience, like many more of their contemporaries then.

The Tudor kings previously had toyed with the notion of separating the Tongue of England from the rest of the Hospital and converting it into a straightforward national force to be specifically employed in the defense of Calais—a costly undertaking which the Order should defray out of its own revenues. Both Henry VIII and his father had in their time received the complimentary title of "Protector of the Order"—no less ironically in the upshot than Henry VIII's other honorary style (conferred by the pope) of "Defender of the Faith." For the Tongue of England was dissolved by Act of Parliament in 1540, and the ten last English Knights took refuge in the Convent of Malta.

A point, the significance of which will not appear till later, must here be emphasized. The Order, of course, did not and could not recognize an act of forcible dissolution by any authority other than the Knights' sole suzerain, the pope; and the English Tongue, therefore, continued extant in principle at its Auberge on Malta.

Here, in 1565, the last resounding victory of St. John's arms was won. Sultan Suleiman the Magnificent, the conqueror of Rhodes, in his old age desired to accomplish the final expulsion of the Order from the eastern Mediterranean and launched a massed attack on the Maltese islands. In command of the Knights was a second old man, the Grand Master Jean de la Valette, seventy-one years of age but combining "the fighting energy of a youth with the wisdom and experience of age." To his strength of character was later attributed the principal part in the repulse of the Turks, and the Maltese city of Valletta is his monument.

No, it was not the Turks who drove the Order from its last territorial stronghold. Just as it had not been the Infidel who

TEXT CONTINUED ON PAGE 68

CONSILIUM
IN
ARENA

THE GRAND COUNCIL AT MALTA

This painting by Giovanni Battista Tiepolo shows the Knights in the council hall of the Grand Master's Palace at Valletta in 1740. The occasion is the appearance of two counts from Udine, a town north of Venice, to request that the noble fam-ilies of their town be admitted to the Order. One of them com-missioned Tiepolo to record the scene: the Grand Master, the two petitioners, the Knights and their guests, are all rendered in the great tradition of Venetian pageant painting.

TEXT CONTINUED FROM PAGE 65

put an end to the Order of the Templars, the instrument of destruction came from France. In 1798, on his way to Egypt, Napoleon anchored the French Fleet off Malta, demanding immediate surrender. Under the irresolute rule of the Grand Master Ferdinand von Hompesch—seventy-first in a line of men usually of other stamp—the Knights capitulated and abandoned their home without any attempt at resistance.

In France itself, the Revolution had already abolished and expropriated the Tongues of Provence, Auvergne, and France, along with other religious fraternities; and it is true that for nearly ten years the Convent of Malta had been acting as one of the main centers of asylum for French aristocrats fleeing from the Revolutionary Terror.

Another such center was in Russia, the only Continental country to remain outside Napoleon's sway. The reigning czar was Paul I, son of Catherine the Great and the mentally unstable Peter III—with a patrimony, thus, of considerable eccentricity. Like certain other secular princes before him, Czar Paul had become fascinated with an ambition to unite in his person both temporal and spiritual dominion. The office of Grand Master to the foremost Order of Military Knights seemed an exemplary springboard. When the bulk of the Maltese refugees accepted an invitation to his court, the Czar's aspirations were realized to the extent that he obtained the Grand Magistry—illegally and without papal approval, as it happened, since Ferdinand von Hompesch was alive in Trieste and only subsequently induced to resign, and his imperial successor was neither a Catholic, nor a professed Knight, nor even unmarried. (Since, however, the continuity of the Order proved to have been saved by the Czar's unstatutory election, he has his place in the list of seventy-six Grand Masters starting with the Blessed Gerard. He is quaintly cited by some as "Fra Paolo Imperatore di Russia.") His dreams ended with his assassination in 1801. For seventy-four years, during most of the nineteenth century, the office of Grand Master was left unfilled.

It looked as if the Order of St. John were at last breaking up. In Poland and Germany the national Tongues no longer subscribed to the Catholic faith. At the fall of Napoleon possession of Malta was awarded to Britain against unavailing representations by the Order, and attempts to regain Rhodes instead also came to nothing. Nor did any hope remain of making good a claim to certain West Indian islands which by cession from Louis XIV had belonged to the Knights for a short time.

But the Order was in process not of dissolution but of transition. Towards the end of the eighteenth century a hybrid Tongue lacking any territorial relationship had come into being with the foundation of the Anglo-Bavarian Order as a separate entity from the German Tongue as such. And in 1831 the English Order was revived, largely by the agency of a commission of French Knights of St. John, whose action was, however, repudiated by the Order's supreme authority in Rome after some twenty years' deliberations. The issue on

The Priory of the Knights of Malta (above left), head quarters of the international Catholic Order, stands the Aventine hill in Rome. When the main door is close

The Knights of St. John have left their mark on both th islands whose names they successively took. The city Rhodes (above left), with its great walls and its Stree

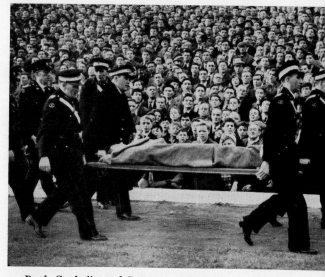

Both Catholic and Protestant Orders are devoted to bat tlefield rescue work in war and to parallel charities i peacetime. In England volunteers of the St. John Ambu

keyhole precisely frames a view, through the garden d across the Tiber, of the dome of St. Peter's. The last and Master of the Order was Price Ludovico Chigi

(center), who died in 1951. His successor has yet to be elected by the Grand Council, seen (above right) in session. The Catholic Knights are members of noble families.

f the Knights, stands today almost as the Hospitallers ft it. Malta (above right) named its capital city Valletta or the Grand Master who led the defense against Turk-

ish siege in 1565. This view, which is seen from the city walls, shows Fort St. Michael and the harbor area, now rebuilt after the savage bombing endured in World War II.

```
52 16      22, v. L. dal Verme ----------------------- 29 83 14
         ORDINE RELIGIOSO CARMELITANI SCALZI,
54 54      Ambulatorio medico, dentistico · 23, p. della
06 88      Scala ------------------------------------- 50 62 45
09 96    ORDINE SOVRANO DI MALTA, cancelleria,
52 23      68, v. Condotti (n. 4 linee urbane con ricerca
09 78      automatica della linea libera) ----------- 68 88 51
45 57      3, p. del Cavalieri di Malta -------------- 59 35 68
49 24      68, v. Bocca di Leone -------------------- 68 72 02
55 65    ORDIONI Andrea (a) 433, v. Appia Nuova ------- 78 64 67
08 80    ORDIONI comm. Cesare (a) 8, v. A. Gallonlo --- 42 41 4 74
12 40    ORDONSELLI Giulio (a) 96, v. G. B. Bodoni ----- 59 52 13
         ORDONSELLI Romoio, laborat idraulico, 3/a, v. Quinto
```

```
" St. John of Jerusalem," 164 St John st EC1..CLErknwl 5840
St. John of Jerusalem Primary School,
                    Ainsworth rd E9...AMHerst 0730
ST. JOHN THE ORDER OF,
                    St. John's gte EC1...CLErknwl 6644
ST. JOHN ORDER OF,Chancery,Opthal Hosp
   Stores Dept,St John's gte EC1.............CLErknwl 6644
   Serv Hosps Welfare VAD Trained Nrses Depts,
              7 Grosvenor cres SW1...BELgravia 6642
   West End Off,Chancery,Pblc Relations SJAA
       Treasury,10 Grosvenor cres SW1...BELgravia 5231
St. John R,31 Willifield wy NW11................SPEedwll 9320
St. John R,Tbcnst,201 Kennington rd SE11......RELiance 1346
```

ance Brigade (above left) carry off a wounded football player. The new building of the Hospital in Jerusalem (above right) opened last fall for the treatment of oph-

thalmic disease. While the Knights still rejoice in medieval ritual, they also respond to numbers prosaically listed in the telephone books of Rome and London (center).

which negotiations foundered was the admission of Protestants to the Tongue of England, a concession without which, it was thought, revival would be doomed to failure in a predominantly Protestant country.

As a military force pure and simple the Hospitallers were an anachronism under modern conditions of war. But their ancient dual tradition of courage under fire and their care of the wounded qualified them to fill a growing need on the battlefields of the nineteenth century. So, under the influence of the libertarian currents released by the French Revolution, of the exigencies of the Napoleonic Wars, and of the swing to authoritarian reaction all over the Continent, the Order of St. John had begun to gain fresh vigor. The battlefields of Europe wanted organized medical services simultaneously as, threatened in their privileges, monarchs and nobility clung with redoubled tenacity to that aspect of medieval chivalry which of old had lent the Military Orders many of the features of an exclusive club.

At the same time the age was one of awakened public conscience towards the sufferings of the poor and sick in ordinary, civic life and in all parts of the globe; and here again the Order of St. John was ready to hand as a vehicle of relief. Its work in the Crimea, and during the Franco-Prussian War, was matched by its many new foundations to aid the diseased and disabled, from any cause, of any class, creed, and race—and this applies to both the international Catholic organization (The Sovereign Order of Malta) and the English Protestant organization (The Most Venerable Order of the Hospital of St. John of Jerusalem).

Both the Sovereign Order and the Venerable Order promptly associated themselves with the Red Cross societies born of the Geneva Convention of 1864, at which the automatic neutrality in war of the wounded and those ministering to them was first formulated. The English branch thereafter gravitated towards ambulance work and first aid.

A large field awaited them at home in the sphere of industrial accidents, for which until then no organized relief had been provided. Also, the ex-servicemen and the war-disabled fast became their especial charges, and, in the form of the St. John Ambulance Association—and Brigade—the organization spread throughout the British Empire and inspired a spate of similar ones in other countries.

In the Catholic Order today only two Tongues exist in fact, those of Italy and Germany, besides the Grand Priory of Bohemia, which at present has only symbolic reality, and a large number of "National Associations." The Catholic Order as a whole has preserved its character as a religious society and its aristocratic orientation. From their headquarters in Rome the Maltese Knights support many institutions—infirmaries, clinics, leper hospitals and blind schools, dispensaries, rest and rehabilitation centers of various kinds—in many other parts of the world besides Italy.

Resurrection of St. John's Hospital at Jerusalem, however, where the Knights' long history had begun, fell to the English Order. The Turkish government was prevailed upon to give permission to establish a new Hospital of St. John in its distant birthplace, now specializing in the treatment of ophthalmic disease, scourge of the Middle East. Hence the onetime pilgrims' hostelry soon became itself a place of pilgrimage for patients from all over Palestine. The Infidel, once the Hospital's designated foe, was strongly represented, the majority of the population being Moslems or Jews. Twice destroyed, in World War I and again in the Arab-Jewish riots after World War II, the Hospital is housed in a new building which opened last fall.

The Sovereign Order particularly distinguished itself during the Hungarian uprising of 1956. Until the frontier was closed, automobile convoys from Austria carried supplies right into Budapest and ambulance trains went back and forth; later, first aid stations and collection centers carried on along the frontier. Homes for Hungarian refugees were set up afterwards.

The ancient forms of military hierarchy and martial trappings are to some extent preserved in both descendants from the medieval stock. Uniforms are worn, not merely on ceremonial occasions. Roughly, the principal three classes of the original structure still obtain, though modified to a greater or lesser degree: greater in the Venerable Order where, for example, the condition of nobility is waived and several of the higher offices are purely honorary, and lesser in the Sovereign Order where, however, the proportion of full, professed Knights is now extremely small compared with former times. The Grand Master of the latter ranks as a sovereign head of state—a landless state but with its governing nucleus resident in Rome; while a sovereign head of state, that is, the reigning English monarch, is the titular head of the Protestant Order of St. John in England.

It has been a long journey, along a road which has been fairly straight, all things considered, and which as far as human eye can see goes on extending so into the future.

Novelist, translator, and devoted student of history, Edith Simon has most recently published The Piebald Standard: A Biography of the Knights Templars *(1959).*

A RENAISSANCE KNIGHT

This ideal Knight of St. John, kneeling in an ideal Renaissance landscape, was painted by Pinturicchio about 1504. It is meant to be a portrait in youth of Alberto Arringhieri, who became the rector of Siena Cathedral. Since it was commissioned in this Knight's old age, it is notable not as a likeness of the subject but as a representation of the Order's garb and a reminder of its long dedication to the service of Christ.

On Stage: LEONTYNE PRICE

When assessing the operatic stage, Leontyne Price, the handsomely gifted thirty-four-year-old American soprano, is given to remarks that distinguish her from her European colleagues in somewhat the manner of a baseball fan who has wandered in full cry into a cricket match. "Maria Callas," she remarks, "was like a cotton-pickin' hypodermic needle for opera." Or, of her own highly successful debut at the San Francisco Opera, she recalls, "I enjoyed a real cold petrification." Miss Price, if with less spectacular results than Callas, has of course been something of a hypodermic for opera herself, and her enthusiasm for a career whose success was confirmed this season with a debut at the Metropolitan Opera (as Leonora in *Il Trovatore*), is both highly vocal ("I really did it in Salzburg, dear") and flavored with the slightly irreverent overtones that Americans often assume in the presence of grand opera.

All of which is not to say that she is anything but deadly serious about her career. She is, by the testimony of conductors and others who have worked with her, a dedicated and a superbly intuitive singer, one who is able to achieve an almost visceral communion with the gaudy passions of *dramma per musica*. At the service of this intuition is a voice that has power and impressive range and that, particularly in its upper register, glows with a fitfully dramatic fever. Technically, Miss Price is a *spinto*—that is, a lyric soprano with a dramatic quality—and consequently she has enough vocal flexibility to tackle dramatic roles like Cio-Cio-San in *Butterfly* and Leonora in *Trovatore*, together with the more lyric flights of Pamina in *The Magic Flute* or, say, the Verdi *Requiem*. The role in which she has most conspicuously distinguished herself so far is that *spinto* classic, Aïda. When she made her debut at La Scala last spring as the Ethiopian slave girl, she moved her audience—particularly in the third-act aria "O cieli azzurri," in which she made the ascent to high C in a pianissimo swelling into forte—to Latinate frenzies normally reserved for only the most favored of home-grown talent. The impact of her performance was enhanced by her appearance: Miss Price has a broad, flat-planed face that carries extraordinarily well across the footlights, and her carriage is impeccably regal. Moreover, as Aïda she wore a white gathered floor-length gown with a single strap, which left scant doubt that she possesses one of the stateliest figures in grand opera. The effect on Milanese music critics was devastating. "Intelligence and sensitivity glow from her magnificent skin," wrote one; another was astounded that Miss Price "mysteriously recalls through her blood the desert and the Sphinx."

The line of descent between the Sphinx and Miss Price is at best a tenuous one. Born in Laurel, Mississippi (her father was a sawmill laborer, her mother a midwife), she started studying piano with the aid and encouragement of a well-to-do local family. When she got to Central State College in Ohio, Miss Price and her teachers discovered roughly simultaneously that she had a voice. She entered the Juilliard School of Music on a scholarship and got the kind of happy break that has characterized her career: Virgil Thomson heard her in a student production and asked her to appear in a revival of his opera *Four Saints in Three Acts*.

Miss Price (who is married to the singer William Warfield and lives, when she is not on tour, in a "tall, chubby house" in Greenwich Village) is proud of the fact that she is that rarest of commodities, an American grand opera product. "Chauvinistically," she will say, "I'm an American troubador." Her path to the opera house led her through the musical stage—she appeared as Bess in the triumphant international touring company of *Porgy and Bess*—and television, where she made her grand opera debut in the title role of the NBC production of *Tosca*. The progression, she feels, was a perfectly logical one: "Both were strumpets, only Tosca dressed better." Unlike many American singers of her generation, she made her grand opera stage debut in a native opera house—as the prioress in the U.S. première of Poulenc's *Dialogues of the Carmelites* at the San Francisco Opera. (From the beginning, Miss Price has had a strong affinity for contemporary music, and she has given premières of songs by such varied talents as Samuel Barber, Lou Harrison, Wilhelm Killmayer, and Henri Sauguet.) Her immensely successful European career began at the Vienna Staatsoper in 1958, when she appeared in *Aïda* under Herbert von Karajan, who has remained one of her most persistent fans.

In conversation Miss Price prefers to stress her achievements as an American singer rather than as an American Negro singer, but she is powerfully aware of her racial identification and of its significance in her career. Thus she had insisted that she would not make her Metropolitan Opera debut in *Aïda*, although she agreed to sing the role after she had established her credentials in some other part. On the other hand, her attitudes about racial matters can be as broadly mocking as her attitude about the more hallowed conventions of the opera stage. Rudolf Bing explained to her recently that when she tours next spring with the Metropolitan as Minnie in *The Girl of the Golden West,* she might encounter housing difficulties in certain southern towns. Miss Price directed at him an artless brown gaze. "Surely, Mr. Bing," she said, "you can work out something for me and the horse." RICHARD MURPHY

On Stage: GOLD AND FIZDALE

When they are playing, the duo-pianists Arthur Gold and Robert Fizdale are everyone's delight; when they are at a party they are everyone's despair. For the specific things that characterize their work on stage—the qualities that make it perfect—are also carried over to their daily life: to wit, each divines by some super-sixth sense what the other is thinking and feeling. They have been known to start speaking, in different parts of a room, and say exactly the same thing in exactly the same words.

Actually, the success of the team (and it is luminous and international) is directly traceable to their ability to breathe together musically and to share a common vision about the way any given piece should go. Instinctively, there is total agreement on the manner in which a phrase should be shaped, in which a syncopation should be treated, in which, in a complex of musical tissue, a hidden bass or treble line should be brought into prominence. The Gold-Fizdale phenomenon is downright spooky. There is no other word for it.

Now as it happens, the art of duo-piano playing is highly specialized. It is imperative that the performers develop a perfectly matched tone quality in order to preclude the possibility of one player arrogating more attention to himself than to the other, thus upsetting the all-important balance of sonority. Also, they must have what is perhaps describable as a communal technique, for it would hardly do if one member of the team were a dashing virtuoso and the other only moderately dependable in terms of bravura. In these regards, Gold and Fizdale are supreme. If you turn your back on them, it is impossible to distinguish who is playing what. As concerns artistic expressiveness, they are as close to being identical twins as can be found in the whole province of music. Of them Samuel Barber has written the following: "An exception to the usual tiresome anonymity of most two-piano teams is Gold and Fizdale. This is because they have a point of view: about the way they play, about the music they play, about the music especially composed for them. Such a real fusion of two artistic personalities makes their concerts unique."

Duo-pianists are not, by nature, the happiest of men, since they labor under one staggering handicap—their repertory is woefully small as compared to that of, say, a solo pianist. Except for a brief fad of multiple-piano playing in public before the mid-nineteenth century, when Chopin and Liszt participated in gala performances by as many as six players, duo-pianism did not emerge from the salon to the concert hall until about 1920, by which time its standard repertory embraced only a bare handful of classics (including a single Mozart sonata and sets of variations by Schumann and Brahms) supplemented by later works by Saint-Saens, Debussy, Rachmaninoff, Reger, and others. Of the eminent two-piano teams that have concertized since 1920—among them Maier and Pattison, Bartlett and Robertson, Luboshutz and Nemenoff, Josef and Rosina Lhevinne, Whittemore and Lowe, and Vronsky and Babin—many have added arrangements to the literature, and some have had new music written for them. But none can rival Gold and Fizdale's contributions to the repertory. They have commissioned an exceptional number of works by contemporaries—Francis Poulenc, Darius Milhaud, Vittorio Rieti, Paul Bowles, Ned Rorem, John Cage, and others. And when their supply of living composers commences to dwindle, they ransack European libraries in an effort to discover old works that have been hidden under the dust of time. Recently they uncovered, in East Berlin, two unpublished two-piano concertos by no less a figure than Felix Mendelssohn. They promptly offered one of them in what was probably the first performance since Mendelssohn and his sister Fanny, who were duo-pianists by avocation, played it for their own amusement.

It was also for their own amusement that the two young men (Arthur Gold is on the left, Robert Fizdale on the right in the photograph opposite) first began to experiment with two-piano literature. They were fellow students at the Juilliard School of Music, both having gone there to prepare for solo careers. Gold, the elder by one year, had come from Toronto, where at the age of three he had begun to play the piano by ear. Fizdale, a Chicagoan, was a bit more backward—he was six before he began to study. Independently, they had come to have reservations about a future spent in the lonesome pursuits of the solo artist. But once they played together, they discovered a startling capacity for intuiting one another's thoughts; they knew on the spot that they were to share a joint professional destiny.

Together their fortunes have flowered to the point where Gold and Fizdale are widely regarded as the pre-eminent duo-pianists of the world today. "It's a good life, too," Gold remarks. "Bob and I are very gregarious and hate being alone. Now we never are." "And another advantage," adds Fizdale, "is that we are dealing with a repertory that has no rigorous performance tradition behind it. We are on our own, so to speak; I mean we don't copy anyone. The interpretative style we have developed belongs exclusively to us."

Asked to cite any cardinal disadvantage inherent in the two-piano performance, they pause for a moment and stare hard at each other. Suddenly, with that unanimity so symptomatic of them, Gold and Fizdale exclaim: "Disadvantage? Yes! We have to split the fees!"   JAY S. HARRISON

In Poussin's Inspiration of the Poet *(c. 1635), a mythic bard is crowned and inspired by Apollo and the muse Calliope*

POUSSIN

ENTHRONED IN HIS TIME,

LATER ENTOMBED,

THE CLASSIC FRENCH MASTER

NOW SPEAKS ACROSS THE CENTURIES

AS A SPACIOUS INNOVATOR

AND PRECURSOR OF MODERN ART

By PIERRE SCHNEIDER

Poussin's self-portrait, painted in 1650

I

n Marcel Proust's *Remembrance of Things Past,* the snobbish Mme de Cambremer at one point exclaims, "In heaven's name, after a painter like Monet, who is an absolute genius, don't go and mention an old hack without a vestige of talent, like Poussin. I don't mind telling you frankly that I find him the deadliest bore."

As Proust placed it in time, that remark was made about fifty years ago, and it symbolizes the disdain with which Poussin's work was viewed by many people of cultural pretensions, not only then but during the decades before and after. For Poussin, the most renowned of French painters in his own lifetime, has suffered from the most insidious of all evils: an excess of praise. His seventeenth-century contemporaries acclaimed him pompously as "The French Apelles" and "The Raphael of our century." He was embalmed in glory; and, petrified by this kiss of death, he gradually became smothered under accumulating layers of prejudice, ignorance, and yellow varnish.

Yet today we find ourselves amidst a phenomenal revival of interest in, and an admiration for, the art of Poussin, to the point where many critics, assessing in particular the historic exhibition of his work at the Louvre in 1960, have acclaimed him as one of the greatest, if not the very greatest, of all the painters in France's long, illustrious tradition.

So sweeping a reversal of opinion is unusual in art. It suggests that Poussin, creator of those cool, austere, classical compositions and landscapes which at first glance seem so remote from all present-day concerns, nevertheless has something particular to communicate to us today. Long accustomed to regard him as a pious but belated preserver of the Renaissance tradition, we have finally come to recognize in him one of the most influential pioneers of modern art. For this organizer of mythological ballets on canvas also rediscovered nature and in so doing helped create the realistic landscape. This teller of heroic fables, furthermore, foreshadowed abstract painting—as well as the modern craft of cartooning. For he gives us instances both of the former's reliance on purely formal elements and the latter's use of miens to reveal psychological states.

To be sure, fellow artists over the generations have shown themselves more perceptive of Poussin than has a fickle public. A stodgy academician? Yet the fieriest of romantics, Delacroix, called him one of the "boldest innovators in the history of art." Constable ranked him with Rubens, Titian, and Rembrandt as one of the four great masters of landscape. Degas dreamed "of something well made, of a well-ordered whole, in the style of Poussin. . . ." Such widely differing artists as Corot and Gris, Greuze and Seurat, Ingres and Courbet, Daumier and Mondrian, along with Pissarro, Matisse, Picasso, and even Rouault have fed on his art—proof enough that it is unusually rich and substantial. Cézanne, who owed particularly much to him, said, "Every time I come away from Poussin I know better who I am."

Today the obscuring glazes have been removed at last, and *we* know better who Poussin is. In his true light he appears as one of the greatest, most complex and varied of painters. For in seeking to maintain the past, he laid the foundations of the future; indeed, he may well have been the last artist in whom tradition and originality, romance and reality, came to harmonious terms. His *Self-Portrait* (above) may stand as the symbol of this variety: the stern figure of the artist appears against a background composed of frames, as if to underscore the rational, abstract aspect of his talent, but a counterpoint is created by the female figure on the left, her shoulders clasped by unexplained hands, reaffirming, if nothing else, the rights of the imagination and the presence of mystery in a compass-drawn universe. Poussin's work is full of such conflicting tendencies—more exactly, with tendencies that *ought* to be conflicting and that *would* be anywhere but in Poussin's painting.

This many-sidedness, these very contradictions, determine and explain his classicism. For classicism, as Poussin demonstrates, is an effort to mediate between divergent and even antagonistic forces. It is a hard-won equilibrium, unstable as that of a tightrope walker, a precise, pinpoint, juggler's balance, like the spheres which Poussin in his pictures is fond of balancing on top of columns and obelisks. It is this tension that differentiates Poussin's classicism from the baroque as well as from the sheer academic. For one could say that the classic is an unstable equilibrium, whereas the baroque is all instability and the academic is all just equilibrium. The baroque is one-sided, though it carries that side to its magnificent extreme. The academic regards as an end the formulas worked out by the classic to master the chaos of contradictory tendencies; the two are about as alike as a Mozart sonata played by Gieseking and by a mechanical piano. Like the casual smile on the tightrope walker's lips, Poussin's seemingly effortless poise on the divide of several artistic worlds contains a lesson of courage. It is one particularly appropriate today, when the most gifted painters cultivate a specialty and abandon themselves to a single course rather than face up to the difficulty of being caught between conflicting, equally powerful, poles. Poussin accepts the duality. He formulates it in the background of his *Self-Portrait*: NICOLAUS POUSSINUS ANDELYENSIS ACADEMICUS ROMANUS, the inscription begins. Les Andelys, a little Normandy village overlooking the river Seine, where they grow wheat and apples; Rome, the cultural capital of Christendom. These places mark the poles of his life and work. Les Andelys—Rome: peasant and poet.

It was in Les Andelys, or rather in the neighboring hamlet of Villers, that Nicolas Poussin was born in June, 1594, the son of a soldier turned farmer and of a woman of the petty *bourgeoisie*. Very little is known of his early life and career, enough however to give us the picture of a precocious and wholehearted dedication to art and art alone. He had been sent to school but soon found his attention wandering from the text of his Latin primers and history manuals to the margins where he could scribble. An honest craftsman of painting, Quantin Varin, brought to Les Andelys to execute a few commissions, may have given him his first lessons. After Varin's departure, it is said that Poussin ran away from home to Rouen, not for adventure's sake, but to obtain further tutoring in his chosen career. His parents being hostile to his career, he at last left clandestinely for Paris in 1612.

But Paris had not yet become the artistic capital that we know today. In the field of painting, it was distinctly provincial; so much so that when the Queen, Marie de Médicis,

required an artist of real stature to decorate her new mansion, the Palais de Luxembourg, she was forced to summon a foreigner, the Flemish Rubens. The Renaissance, abruptly imported from Florence to Fontainebleau, had interrupted a flourishing national tradition. The French distorted it, diluted it, reduced it to ornamentalism and eclectic mannerism. The exigent Poussin could find little satisfaction in such a climate. He spent a month in the studio of the mediocre Georges Lallemand, three more in that of the uninspired Ferdinand Elle. A young nobleman offered him room, board, and plenty of walls to paint on in his château in Poitou. Poussin followed him there only to discover that the young squire's mother refused to see in him anything but a menial servant. Poussin soon left this hostile house. Destitute, he painted his way back to Paris: an altarpiece here, a shop sign there. He reached the city so starved, so utterly exhausted that he was forced to return to Villers to restore his shaken health. After a year he went back to Paris, no doubt convinced that it could be for him little more than a stepping stone. Seriousness and perseverance already were his dominant traits. Much later, when someone asked him to what cause he attributed his ranking among the most illustrious painters of the times, he replied, "I neglected nothing." Others around him might be satisfied with halfway solutions and shabby substitutes; Poussin wanted to go to the source. And the source, at that time, was Rome.

Twice, he tried to reach it. Twice, lack of money stopped him, the first time in Florence, the second in Lyon. The decisive opportunity was given him in 1624 by a poet, the precious, then vastly famous Marino. The Italian concettist had divined Poussin's genius, had asked him to illustrate his interminable poem, *Adonis*, then invited the painter to join him in Rome. So at last Poussin arrived in the Eternal City.

For a number of years his existence remained a difficult one. Marino, having recommended Poussin to Cardinal Barberini, left for Naples, where he died shortly thereafter. Barberini showed a friendly disposition but left Rome himself on diplomatic mission. Without steady patrons, Poussin lived poorly, on the Via Paolina, selling his paintings for starvation prices. He was a rather isolated stranger—a stranger in French dress, at that, which caused him, one night, to be attacked by the local soldiery and wounded in the wrist; for the French were not popular in the Papal States, at the time favorable to France's enemy, Spain.

After his nocturnal mishap, Poussin adopted Roman dress. In 1630, carrying the assimilation a step further, he took a Roman-born wife, the daughter of a humble pastry cook. Gradually his situation improved. His reputation grew, his prices rose, and he acquired influential patrons, above all Cassiano dal Pozzo, a wealthy nobleman whose erudition and attachment to antiquity left a profound mark on him. Ten years after his arrival Poussin's lean times were over, and the lineaments of his personal style had begun to emerge (see the painting *Tancred and Erminia*, which opens the portfolio of color reproductions accompanying this article.

Poor in material success, those early years had been rich in experience. Rome was the heiress and the successor of the leading centers of the Renaissance: Florence and Venice. The renewed strength and stability of the Church, after the great Protestant schism, impelled the popes to embellish the capital of the Catholic world with monuments illustrating their power and glory. The churches, in continual process of decoration and redecoration, became veritable studios and art galleries. Palaces and villas accumulated the treasures of ancient and renascent art. From this immense reservoir, artists borrowed freely—in those days, imitation was regarded as a virtue rather than a vice—a head here, an attitude there, a drapery from somewhere else, so that the work of uninspired practitioners often looked like a skillfully woven plaid of quotations. This dominant eclecticism was flanked on the one side by the revolutionary realism of Caravaggio and his followers, underlined by their violent highlighting, and on the other by the theatrical pomp of the baroque, developed by Pietro da Cortona, Bernini, Borromini, with its insistence on irregularity, motion, illusionism, and flights of fancy.

Poussin responded vigorously to this wealth of models and incitements. His work, during that phase, is a series of continuous, sometimes contradictory, experiments. He drew after ancient bas-reliefs, but also in the streets of Rome and around it; he copied Titian's bacchanals and illustrated Leonardo's notebooks. In turn dramatic and elegiac, he explored the realm of mythology and chivalrous romance as well as religion; he even displayed on occasion a sensuality so voluptuous that some pictures actually shocked French collectors: one of his Venuses was thus censored beyond recognition.

Few facts are certain about these early paintings, and their very variety makes them difficult to date. Still, the general pattern of Poussin's approach is clear. "I am a serious man," he wrote to the French courtier Chantelou. It is this seriousness that makes him shy away from the emphatic shallowness of Caravaggio and from the surface dazzlement of Pietro da Cortona. He shuns extremism, not out of timidity, but because both extremes attract him equally. Although we tend to view Poussin as a master of form, the paintings of the early 1630's show him to be a glowing colorist in the lineage of Bellini, Giorgione, Veronese, and Titian. He fashioned a relief model in clay of the latter's *Wedding of Aldobrandini*. This quaint undertaking may stand as a symbol of the taxing problems he had set himself: to reconcile Titian's color with Raphael's form. Unlike the eclectics, however, who achieved such a reconciliation by watering down these extreme terms, Poussin went back to the undiluted sources, where their conflict was sharpest. Yet in such masterpieces as *Tancred and Erminia* and *Bacchanal with a Lute Player,* Poussin resolves it. Roman firmness and Venetian mellowness, local color and over-all tonality are intimately wedded in a mood that is solemnly joyous. Thus

Poussin's most richly obscure and many-sided period already produced instances of a classic equilibrium. Anyone less intransigent would gladly have contented himself with so superb a synthesis.

But there was in Poussin's personality a germ which his vigor impelled him to develop, thereby upsetting this first solution and orienting his work into a direction most perilous for a painter. Peasant and poet: like the new townsman anxious to erase all traces of his rustic origins, Poussin increasingly forsakes earthy Andelysian sensibility for learned Roman sense. He becomes *Monsu Pussino,* whose literary erudition was much admired. His friends and patrons no doubt encouraged him to follow this bent: Marino, who made him read Ovid; Pozzo, in whose library he could study books on perspective, geometry, optics, architecture, and anatomy and meet learned persons. Had not his beloved Raphael manifested his own intellectualism by glorifying, in painting, the *"certa idea"*? Poussin's admiration for the severe Domenichino worked in the same direction. Domenichino had once declared, "No line not previously shaped in the mind must come from the painter's hand."

Poussin's own hand periodically issued its warning. "If [only] the hand would obey me . . ." he writes. "[But] I do not lose courage, for, as long as the head shall function properly (though its servant be feeble) it will always make it respect the best and most excellent parts of its profession." Everything, in short, conspired to make Poussin subject by all possible means the act of painting to the will of the intellect. Looking at his *Phocion's Ashes,* Bernini tapped his forehead and remarked, "He is a painter who works from here." Poussin himself declared that "a painter is not great if he only imitates what he sees," and added "skillful persons must work from the Intellect."

Elsewhere, he informs Chantelou about a projected painting: "Its idea is settled upon, which is the main thing." Nowhere is this gradual retreat of instinct before thought, of spontaneity before calculation, more evident than in his drawings. Watching a work from first to final sketch, we can follow with what thoroughness he applies to his raw material "the office of reason." In the successive steps of *The Judgment of Solomon* (pages 92, 93), for instance, all picturesque incidentals are gradually removed, till only the heart of the drama remains visible. Man's mind triumphing over matter: this is the very quintessence of the humanist attitude; and the definition of painting which Poussin gives at this stage conforms strictly to the humanist ideal. "Painting is nothing else than the imitation of human actions . . . ; the others should not be imitated in themselves, except by accident, and not as main elements but as accessories; and in this manner may be imitated not only the actions of animals, but all natural things."

The ideal is clear. Painting, as one of Poussin's admirers put it, must "talk." A canvas should not only be visible to the eye but legible to the mind. Listing the components of

TEXT CONTINUED ON PAGE 89

THE NOBLE VOICE OF NICHOLAS POUSSIN

A PORTFOLIO

TANCRED AND ERMINIA, c. 1635

Above: The subject of this masterpiece of Poussin's early years in Rome was taken from Tasso's epic of the Crusades, *Jerusalem Delivered*. The Syrian Erminia, in love with Tancred, finds him fallen in combat. While his lieutenant, Vafrin, supports him, she cuts off her hair to stanch his bleeding.

ORPHEUS AND EURYDICE, c. 1650

Overleaf, Plate One: While the divine lyrist (right foreground) woos his bride among her maidens, a passer-by standing between him and Eurydice conceals her from his sight just as she is fatally stung by a viper. An enchanted landscape surrounds the scene: in rear, Rome's Castel Sant' Angelo.

SUMMER, OR RUTH AND BOAZ, 1660–64

Overleaf, Plate Two: In painting for the Duc de Richelieu a cycle on the four seasons that formed the climax of his work, Poussin chose for *Summer* the Biblical story of Ruth, who appears (foreground) kneeling before Boaz as he orders a servant (right) to rejoin the other gleaners of his grain.

LANDSCAPE WITH POLYPHEMUS, 1649

THE ENTOMBMENT, c. 1650

Preceding Two Pages: Atop a Sicilian crag sits the lovelorn Cyclops, playing pipes for the absent sea-nymph Galatea. Myth and allegory are mixed: monstrous Polyphemus personifies primitive life; nearer, the earth is cultivated; in foreground, nymphs and satyrs embody secret, fruitful springs of nature.

Above: Of Poussin's many paintings on Old and New Testament subjects, this is one of the most dramatic. The Virgin and other mourners familiar to Western painting are shown about the body of Christ in postures echoing those of late-Renaissance masters, but with a depth and fervor Poussin's own.

TEXT CONTINUED FROM PAGE 80

his painting *Manna*, Poussin concludes: "all which things, if I am not mistaken, will not be displeasing to those who can *read* them." Then he says: "just as the twenty-six letters of the alphabet serve to formulate our words and to express our thoughts, so the lineaments of the human body serve to express the soul's passions and to show outside what is in one's mind."

Of all the varieties of matter, the human form is the most faithful conductor of the mental message, the best actor in thought's play. Poussin's paintings therefore begin to look literally like a stage on which a dramatic event takes place. Indeed, Poussin took to working out his pictures in three dimensions: he had built a miniature stage on which he set up small wax figures. He then could study distance, relationships, attitudes, folds of dress, and even, by means of lattices behind which he placed candles, the play of light. Hence the waxen, *tableau vivant* air that tends to overtake many works of that period.

With relentless logic he carried the process of rationalization still further. Remembering that Cicero had called gestures "the language of the body," he turned them into a downright semaphore. To make his pictures still more "understandable," he specified the characters' expressions with such precision that fear, anger, joy, or any emotion could be deciphered with ease on the faces of his heroes. A contemporary commentator went so far as to claim that you could tell from the faces of the bystanders in his *Baptism of Christ* that a Voice was speaking to them from heaven. Only a short step was required to standardize this repertory of "faces" into a veritable code. The academician Le Brun, Poussin's disciple, took it. "The eyebrow," he explains gravely, "is the part of the face where the passions show themselves best." Take fright, for instance: "Terror, when it is excessive, causeth the Eye-brow to be very much raised in the middle, and the muscles, which perform the motion of these Parts, very much marked and swelled, and pressed one against another, being drawn down over the Nose, which will seem to be drawn up, as also the Nostrils; the Eyes ought to appear entirely open; the upper Eye-lid hid under the Brow; the White of the Eye ought to be environed with red; etc." Drop the eyebrow, lift the lips, and you get surprise, anger, mirth. . . . This manual by Poussin's disciple, with its handy recipes for the depiction of states of mind, moods, feelings, became as regular a stand-by for the academic painters of the next two centuries as Escoffier's cookbook was to be for chefs. It found its ultimate use in caricature: one wonders whether the creators of Li'l Abner or Mickey Mouse suspect how much they owe to the severe Poussin.

"To introduce judgment everywhere," was his aim, and he neglected nothing. Like a film director obsessed with authenticity, he made certain that every prop, every detail, was plausible and historically correct. In his eagerness to make painting talk, he multiplied allegorical figures as in *Landscape with Polyphemus* (see portfolio). His river-gods, as

one of his collectors remarked impatiently, are like "signs the painter places in the picture to make his meaning clearer." Poussin became incredibly expert at such signaling. No wonder the learned members of the Academy could spend endless hours "reading" the *Manna*! The danger inherent in Poussin's fanatical purpose is obvious: it could—it sometimes almost does—make him the world's most insufferable painter. He would have achieved this dubious distinction had he had his way: his favorite among his own pictures was *The Judgment of Solomon,* a work so frozen that it justifies even Madame de Cambremer's yawn. Poussin was spared this fate. "Sometimes we would be lost if we weren't lost," he once remarked. What saved him was that things got out of hand.

He had striven for correctness, propriety, verisimilitude; yet he found himself exposed to almost grotesque misunderstandings. One critic pointed out that in the *Manna* he had given the Jews a starved look, although according to the Bible they had feasted on a miraculous flight of quail the previous day. Another carped at the omission of the camel in *Eliezer and Rebecca*. In short, Poussin's reason got him trapped in fantasy. His striving for legibility backfired: the pious Madame du Housset, who owned the Vergilian *Shepherds of Arcady,* had placed it in her chapel thinking it was an altarpiece.

Poussin had been caught at his own game, but only because he had played it so very seriously. Thereby, he brought to light the contradictions latent in his procedure; and the very act of facing them honestly carried him beyond the limits before which other artists were brought up short. Poussin's radicalism forced him to realize that action and thought were incompatible. Action is movement, a passing, an appearance; thought is stable, immobile, essential. A gesture, even rationalized and idealized, is not an eternal truth but an awkwardly frozen moment. Hence Poussin now tries to reduce action to immobility. The canvas remains a stage, but it shrinks, and the actors become fewer. A new problem must now be solved: how to reconcile the old need for expression with the new demand for fixity. The answer is masks, which are both meaningful and motionless. The faces of the protagonists now seem covered by plaster casts taken from ancient sculpture. Another answer consists in transforming the drama, in taking it from the physical to the interior, or psychological, level. The limbs quiet down; the eyes become the sole instruments of action, and action gradually gives way to contemplation.

Contemplation was the prime occupation of the Greek gods; and the Olympians were, along with the Holy Family, Poussin's favorite subjects. For us, accustomed by contemporary painting to disregard subjects or at least to consider them as pretexts, it is, perhaps, not easy to realize their importance to the classic master. For him, they must be fully appropriate to his aesthetic and moral preoccupations. "I am not a light person, nor changing in my affections, once I have placed them in a subject." His subjects are in every sense

A vigorous draftsman, Poussin expressed himself with freedom in this early sketch, The Triumph of Galatea, *possibly with a painting in prospect. But no resulting canvas is known.*

loaded. When asked by a collector to execute a *Christ bearing the Cross* as a pendant to a *Crucifixion*, he refused: "I no longer have enough joy or health to engage in these sad subjects. The *Crucifixion* made me ill, a *Bearing* would finish me off." His choice of themes is as significant as are his abstentions. If the Old Testament themes give way little by little to New Testament ones (such as *The Entombment*, see portfolio), and if his Moseses are outnumbered by his Madonnas, it is because physical action prevails in the former, psychological nonaction in the latter. The growing concern with immobility finds a fitting outlet in the themes, so frequent in Poussin's later years, of his *Rest during the Flight into Egypt* and of *The Holy Family,* as it does in the unruffled serenity of his Olympians. Subject matter thus underscores the total reconcilement of aesthetics with religious belief and philosophic thought.

For the Hellenic deities do not in Poussin's eyes conflict with God. To his syncretic mind, Christ might well have been the last of the Greek divinities, a latter-day Apollo—as indeed He appears on the early Christian sarcophagi that Poussin could see in Rome.

This much is sure: Poussin took his gods seriously. His was, in Sir Joshua Reynolds's words, "a mind thrown back two thousand years, and as it were naturalized in antiquity." For him antiquity was no thing of the past: there are no ruins in his work. In Poussin's day everybody invoked the ancients, as today everyone invokes democracy. Unlike that of his contemporaries, however, Poussin's homage was no lip service. Where they saw but a convenient reservoir of mythological ornaments, he recognized pregnant myths.

This difference in spiritual temperature is brought to light by the sojourn of Poussin in France from 1640 to 1642. It

had begun triumphantly. Called back by King Louis XIII of France, who was desirous of lending his reign greater artistic luster, Poussin had been appointed official First Painter. Soon, however, his situation deteriorated, till he searched for a pretext to return to Rome. The underlying reason for his discontent was the role which had been assigned to him: that of a decorator and supervisor of royal pomp—precisely the function which Le Brun, a generation later, was to fill at the court of Louis XIV. Poussin could not fit into such a scheme, no matter how grand. A solitary figure in Paris as in Rome, he was determined to work out his problems, if need be modestly, but in liberty. He was never really successful at painting on a large scale—on the walls of a palace or a church, where his will had to bend before an over-all plan. His preference ran to the relatively small-sized easel painting, executed in the isolation of his studio, which collectors could then purchase. He was to be commissioned, not commanded. Within the limited expanse of easel painting, the truths Poussin wished to render suffered least from dilution. That is the significance of the warning which accompanies a picture sent to Chantelou: "When you receive yours, I beg you, if you find it good, to surround it with a corniced frame, for it needs it, so that, considering it in all its parts, the eye's rays be held together instead of being dispersed outside by taking in the sight of nearby objects which, mixing with those depicted, blur the light." Poussin went back to Rome because Paris wanted to strip the cornice off his pictorial universe.

Once again he resumed the routine which he was to keep till shortly before his death, on November 19, 1665: rising early; walking an hour or two, usually on the Pincio, surrounded by acquaintances who listened attentively to his pronouncements on art; working till evening, when he would go out again and mingle with the people conversing on the Piazza di Spagna. His fame, by now, was immense. His paintings brought the highest prices in Rome, and at that, would-be buyers had to wait for at least two years. Yet Poussin lived with a simplicity worthy of the ancient Stoics whose philosophy increasingly preoccupied him. To a Roman prelate who pitied him for not having even one servant, he replied: "It is I who pity you, Monsignor, for having many." He might have lived royally by painting; he chose to live humbly for it. Nothing could distract him from the perfecting of his art, which acquired an ever more rigorous gravity as it shifted from violent, human action to immobile, Olympian contemplation.

Indeed, the gods are our best guides to the comprehension of this change. Of them Aristotle wrote, "all that concerns action can only seem petty and unworthy." They embody absolute virtue, pure essences, eternal being and so engage only in contemplation—*theōria*, as the Greeks named it—of the order that governs all things and beings. For the Greeks, this order, or *kosmos*, was mathematical: contemplation was, in every sense, theoretical. What gave consistency to worldly appearances and actions was the underlying essences and their relations: mathematical figures and rhythms. Break open the Golden Apple; inside it, you will find the Golden Section.

Such, precisely, is the road followed by Poussin in his radicalism: pure action led him to pure reason, and storytelling to geometrical statement. Some drawings show that he could rival Mondrian in his quest for abstract geometrical truth. And while the time in which he lived prevented him from aspiring overtly toward a solution so extreme in his paintings, he reaches the brink of it by infinitely subtle means in pictures such as *The Confirmation,* which leave our eye to face a symphony of hieratic forms, essential lines, and contrapuntal rhythms. In such canvases Poussin carries out better than Gauguin himself Gauguin's program: "I obtain by arrangements of lines and colors, using as pretext some subject borrowed from human life or nature, symphonies, harmonies that represent nothing real in the vulgar sense of the word; they express no idea directly, but they should make you think as music does, without ideas or images, simply by the mysterious relationships existing between our brains and such arrangements of colors and lines." That is undoubtedly what Bernini meant when, gazing at *The Confirmation,* he said, "What silence!" Poussin had come a long way indeed from "talking painting."

As Mondrian himself and many others have proved, mathematical perfection has a finality which is often fatal to art. That was the danger now threatening Poussin. What saved him was the reappearance, around 1650, of a side of his personality long suppressed: that of the peasant. The first painter who heeded Cézanne's advice to "remake Poussin after nature" was Poussin himself.

Actually Poussin had not altogether excluded nature; he had simply relegated it to the background. Usually he was satisfied to borrow from Bellini or Titian a conventional diagram of tree trunks and cloud-swept skies. Yet even when he devoted special care to landscape, treating it with a delicate firmness that foreshadowed Corot, it remained a backdrop, a screen to close off the dramatic stage. Nature did not yet dare to step up to the footlights. It signaled to us indirectly, through the paintings' subjects.

But in about 1650 nature in Poussin's work rose from the status of "extra" to that of full-fledged protagonist. There was no abrupt reversal, no change of heart or mind; it is absurd to attribute it to purely external influences, such as the fact that Claude Lorrain had just become his neighbor. Poussin, as he said, was not changing in his affections. Quite the contrary, it was once again loyalty to the very values in which he had placed his faith that brought about this drastic transformation.

His values remained the gods, who were eternal, and order, which was geometrical. But according to the Greeks themselves, the gods were the children of the primal goddess, Gaea, that is, earth. Ultimately they derived the fullness of their being from nature. When a young nobleman from

His geometric interest appears in the monumental triangle formed by the chief figures in this drawing for a painting of the Holy Family. Ruled squares were aids for enlargement.

France asked him what antique souvenir he might take back home, Poussin picked up a fistful of dust and, handing it to him, replied, "Take it, milord; this is antiquity." The cult of the ancient gods leads to nature.

So does geometry, whose etymology yields the meaning "the measuring of earth." Never was this truer than in the heyday of Cartesian thought. For, according to Descartes, space and geometry are one. Order, therefore, not only explains reality: it is reality. Measurement *is* earth. Poussin did not go quite so far. But if we look at *Orpheus and Eurydice* (see portfolio) with its many levels of landscape, or his *Landscape of Ancient Rome,* in which a compass-drawn road wedges like an icebreaker into the virgin expanse of space, we see how geometry literally led him into nature. How far that road made him travel can be assessed by comparing his new definition of painting with his earlier one: "It is an imitation, by means of lines and colors, upon a certain surface, of all that is visible under the sun." A long way indeed for a man who, ten years earlier, would certainly have subscribed to the opinion of the satirist Lucian: "It is not valleys and mountains that I look for in paintings, it is men who act and think."

Poussin, who had no intention of abjuring his previous position, thus found himself facing a new problem: how to reconcile figures and landscape, man and nature. To a medieval artist, this would have been no problem, for a common denominator existed between the two terms: God, from whom both creatures and creation derived their life. With the Renaissance, however, the tight theological order collapsed. The link between man and nature being sundered, they went their respective ways, strangers to each other. Human action tended to unfold on a closed stage; creation re-

The development of a Poussin concept from sketch to finished painting is illustrated by the stages of his Judgment of Solomon, *based on the story in I Kings 3:16-28. In the first drawing Solomon is larger than life-sized, the composition turbulent, the architecture dramatic; in the second the atmosphere is more formal and classic, and the painting further refines it.*

treated into the noncommittal, almost hostile silence of the still life. When man and nature now met, it was usually at the expense of the latter; and on the rare occasions when nature was not played down, the figures and the landscapes belonged to worlds so widely apart that the former seemed cut out and pasted on the latter. Some artists had tried to close the gap, that is, to master the middle ground. One answer, stated by Paul Bril, the Flemish landscapist (Poussin's predecessor and, like him, settled in Rome), had been to break it up into successive layers of planes, each delimited by figures, trees, hills, or mountains, and the sum of which composed space as a whole. Giorgione and Titian, on the other hand, had achieved unity of the foreground and the background by subjecting them both to a dominant tone, a uniform key—as two singers separated by the width of the stage are brought together by the duet in which they join.

The intransigent Poussin must have thought these solutions based on approximations, dilutions, compromises. His own bridge was mathematics, the common denominator between human action and landscape. It was no new belief: the Stoics had held the theory that the same law governed both men and nature. "Truth," said Poussin's younger contemporary Malebranche, "is nothing but a relation, either of equality or of inequality." And he formulated the Stoic creed in modern, mathematical terms: "Every grandeur being a relation, and every relation being a grandeur, it is evident that one may express all relations by numbers and represent them to the imagination by lines." Now, if we bear in mind that *grandeur*, in French, means both physical quantity and moral quality—size and greatness—we can see how the same abstract order might serve to define both human and natural relations. In *Eliezer and Rebecca*, for example, the maiden carrying a round jar on her head is echoed faithfully by the column bearing a sphere. And this brings to mind Poussin's half-joking advice to his patron Chantelou, about to visit Nîmes, not only to look at the classic columns of the Maison Carrée but also at the pretty girls, for after all, "the

former are merely old copies of the latter." In Poussin's later works, and particularly in the numerous versions of the Holy Family, the underlying order of the human groups is emphasized by the geometric clarity of the architectural setting, which also brings out the structure of the landscape. The freestanding columns, pyramids, obelisks, and monumental amphoras which recur so often in Poussin's paintings are materializations of the sphere, cone, and cylinder upon which, according to Cézanne, everything in nature is modeled.

Just as it abstracts the figures in the foreground, Poussin's geometry opens up nature in the background. The narrow, dramatic stage now gives way to a landscape so vast that, as someone once noted, it would take more than a day to cross it on foot. Poussin's landscape is unraveled by roads that force the eye to explore it in repeated diagonals, thereby not only lending a feeling of ampleness to canvases of small dimensions, but laying out his earth's anatomy—and one is reminded of Goethe's remark that he could never understand a landscape until he knew its geological constitution.

This new, enormous room is, for the first and only time in the history of art, unbroken. The impact of a group assembled in the foreground is carried to the remotest reaches by the presence, in the distance, of a group similarly cadenced. Rhythms and parallels animate the entire space with carefully calculated echoes and reverberations. The river is still there; indeed, the rivers themselves, through their crystal tranquility, turn into bridges by reflecting, magnifying, and prolonging shapes and colors from the one bank to the other. Thus Orpheus playing to Eurydice on the close shore, the bathers on the other, and the earth all around them participate in a single concert, a composition in the truest sense, directed by that invisible wand: the ruler.

For Poussin, however, mathematical order is a means, not an end. It reconciled in him the poet and the peasant; but once the service was performed, it retreated discreetly, leaving them face to face. And now the peasant had his revenge, not by rejecting the poet's world, but by transposing it, by

rephrasing it in natural, almost homely terms. Orpheus strok-
ing the lyre becomes a farmer playing his bagpipes; the
horses that once drew Apollo's chariot now pull the plow
(see *Summer, or Ruth and Boaz*, in portfolio). In the fili-
gree, so to say, of the dry Roman countryside reappears the
verdant richness of Normandy, which Poussin had left nearly
fifty years before. Rivers had always been a favorite theme
for the artist, raised on the banks of the Seine. Now, in his
late work, cliffs reminiscent of those near Les Andelys rise
up on the Tiberine shores, and in the Castel Sant' Angelo
as painted into *Orpheus and Eurydice* we perceive a reminis-
cence of the Château Gaillard, the stronghold of Richard the
Lion-Hearted. The vegetation, too, becomes thicker, moister,
and the apple trees in *Spring* and *Autumn* are the pride of a
Norman orchard.

The infiltration of Andelysian luxuriance into Roman se-
verity marks nature's triumph in Poussin's ultimate works
(1658–1664). As action had once been reduced to immobility, so now it is absorbed by nature's serenity. Time is swal-
lowed by space, history tapers off into cosmic indifference.
Stoicism gives way to, or rather broadens into, a kind of
pan-naturalism. Poussin, who had found in the arid, vegeta-
tionless abstraction of the Mediterranean city an excellent
model for the stage on which to parade his humanist truths,
now discovered that, in Vauban's words, "the truth is green."

In the paintings of his last years, nature's green truth
rules supreme. Men, beasts, and even demigods are drowned
in its mounting tide. Once the custodians of perfect propor-
tions, they have been thrown out of scale by the dispropor-
tion of nature. Too big or too small, they become transparent
or nearly invisible: Polyphemus so huge that he appears to
be part of the rock on which he sits; Hercules so small that
he is dwarfed by the cliff on which he stands; Orion so
towering that we do not even think of looking for him in the
landscape through which he strides. It takes a while to recognize them, as it does to see things in a dark room when
one enters it coming from a brightly lit one. Nor is this as-

similation of actors, human or divine, by nature the result
merely of technical devices. Simply, the presence of the green
truth has become so overwhelming that it reduces the
dramatis personae, in the words of Andrew Marvell, "to a
green thought in a green shade."

If the baroque is disequilibrium, these landscapes could
be called baroque, for in them nature surges and swells as
the gigantic grapes in *Autumn*. Like a python, it swallows
man and myth. In fact, pythons and other serpents occur
frequently in Poussin's later work as symbols of nature's
sometimes dangerous power over humans. Ultimately, however, nature is beyond good and evil; gods and men, every
creature and thing are at once illumined and submerged, in
Summer, as by the pure light of the first day. More than
color and form, it is this light which imparts to everything,
as Hazlitt said, "that unimpaired look of original nature, full,
solid, large, luxuriant, teeming with life and power."

Never, until Poussin's four paintings of the seasons, had
that unimpaired look of pristine freshness and vastness been
captured so thoroughly by Western painting. In these works,
the fertility of field and meadow, the denseness of foliage,
the sun's rays, and the cloud's rain are inexhaustible. These
paintings are windows opened on a promised land. After
Poussin, it revealed itself again to a Corot, a Courbet, a
Monet, artists who, to paraphrase Bernini, worked from the
eye, the belly, and the heart. What is unique in Poussin's
case is that he worked from the head. Like a surveyor so
engrossed in his measurements that he wanders into the
thick of the jungle, Poussin's abtract conceptions led him
into the heart of concreteness. His friend Claude Lorrain
came to nature ready to love it; he flattered it, pampered it,
sentimentalized it, and sang a pretty song about it. The
grave Poussin accepted its unfathomable, nourishing silence.

---

*Pierre Schneider, an American art critic and free lance living
in Paris, wrote on Joan Miró in the March, 1959,* HORIZON.

BOOKS

The Bible is given New Speech

An important new English translation of the Bible is being made. This month there will appear in modern speech and form the New Testament of the New English Bible; the Old Testament and the books called the Apocrypha will follow in a few years. The enterprise was planned by the chief Protestant churches of Great Britain, whose representatives started work on it some fifteen years ago, with an English bishop as chairman and a Scottish divine as secretary. The delicate work of printing and the solid work of publication are handsomely executed by the University presses of Oxford and Cambridge.

The word Bible means simply "books." One of the difficulties that many readers have felt in understanding the Bible has always been that it does not *look* like a book or a collection of books intended to be read in the regular way. It does not—in the traditional versions—lie normally upon the page, but is set out in narrow columns, often hedged in by notes and variants. Its sentences, instead of running on in continuous narrative or discourse, are often arranged separately and numbered off—15, 16, 17—like chemical formulas. Its punctuation looks odd, with no quotation marks, with irrational capital letters, and with italics used not, as is customary, for emphasis but to mark words which are not in the original and have been supplied by the translators in order to fill out the sense. ("Hail, *thou that art* highly favored, the Lord *is* with thee: blessed *art* thou among women.")

This new translation re-creates the New Testament in the form of a normal book. This has been done before (e.g., in Ernest Sutherland Bates's presentation of the King James Version, *The Bible Designed to be Read as Living Literature*) and should now offend no one. There are, in the original Greek Testament, no numbered "verses." The verse divisions and the numbers were both introduced by a publisher, the Frenchman Henri Estienne (or "Stephanus") in the sixteenth century. They were meant as a convenience. They are now, for most readers, an interference. The stiff old punctuation of the English-language Bibles we read in our childhood was that of the King James translators, which to our eyes lacks both grace and clarity. It was they also who inserted the italics, because their theory of translation was that each word of the original must without fail be represented by one or more words of their English version, otherwise they would be mutilating the word of God; and that any English words added to make the meaning clear must be distinguished from the rest, so that no human addition would profane the word of God. This word-for-word theory was applied, perhaps even invented, by the Jewish translators who turned the Old Testament into Greek for the use of their Greek-speaking co-religionists in Egypt and elsewhere (the Septuagint), because they believed that not only the book, but every word, every letter in it was sacred. Later Saint Jerome adhered to the theory when he made the standard Latin version of the Scriptures, which we call the Vulgate. But the structure of the Greek language, and still more of the Hebrew language, is so different from that of English that it is impossible to translate from one to the other, word for word, and a mistake even to try, because meaning is conveyed not in single words but in groups of words: the true translator considers a sentence in his text, and rather than follow it mechanically element by element, tries to discover or to construct a pattern of words which, in his own tongue, will carry the same total meaning.

This new translation is in the English of today. It can be understood at once, and (as far as language will take us) completely. The King James Version used by many English-speaking Protestants is couched in language which is usually grand, harmonious, and memorable but is sometimes almost incomprehensible nowadays, as when it makes David pray to the Lord to "enlarge his feet" and frequently falsifies the tone and texture of the original. Even the Revised Standard Version published in 1952, although a great improvement on the baroque prose of 1611, is not, and does not claim to be, "a new translation in the language of today." It is usually clear and always dignified, but its style is sometimes too lofty—and sometimes, even as revised, too archaic—to render the New Testament as it was first written and first read. The Gospels and the Acts and some of the Letters in the New Testament are written in a simple straightforward style—so simple, often, that it embarrassed the intellectuals among the early Christians. Their critics asked if a divine message would really be conveyed to mankind in a style so clumsy, so graceless, so close to barbarism. A true translation of these books of the Bible must therefore be plain and straightforward, even bare.

Soon after Paul reached Jerusalem on his missionary journey, he was arrested and taken to Caesarea, the seat of the Roman governor of Judaea. The high priest of the Jews prosecuted him on a charge which, although not closely defined, amounted to "disturbing the peace." What the prosecuting attorney said to the presiding Roman official is given in Acts 24:2-8. Here, in the new translation, is the opening of his speech:

Your Excellency, we owe it to you that we enjoy unbroken peace. It is due to your provident care that, in all kinds of ways and in all sorts of places, improvements are being made for the good of this province. We welcome this, sir, most gratefully. And now, not to take up too much of your time, I crave your indulgence for a brief statement of our case.

This sounds like a speech that might be made in modern times, complimentary but not too flowery (and, after all, it has been abridged in the Acts). I still think this translation is too flaccid, but it has

the smooth rhetorical tone of the original Greek. With it, compare the King James Version:

Seeing that by thee we enjoy great quietness, and that very worthy deeds are done unto this nation by thy providence, we accept *it* always, and in all places, most noble Felix, with thankfulness. Notwithstanding, that I be not further tedious unto thee, I pray thee that thou wouldest hear us of thy clemency a few words.

Three hundred years ago this was probably correct in tone for an advocate representing a subject people and addressing a representative of the occupying power. "Great quietness," however, is a poor rendering of the Greek: the speaker was praising the Romans for maintaining widespread and long-lasting peace.

"Providence" was acceptable in 1611 for "human foresight," although now it is not. "Very worthy deeds are done unto this nation" is a blurred echo of the original. There is no doubt which of the two translations of this passage is more natural and more intelligible for our time.

Ronald Knox thought long and carefully about the problem of translating the Bible, and in one of his last works, the Romanes Lecture given in Oxford in 1957, he analyzed the translator's difficulties with wit and percipience. Yet he did not choose, or dare, to abandon all the conventions which bound English translators of the Bible during the preceding three centuries. His rendering of the attorney's opening paragraph (as given in his version of the New Testa-

---

THE NEW TESTAMENT BECOMES NEWER:
FOUR VERSIONS OF THREE GOSPELS

	MATTHEW 5:37	LUKE 21:36	JOHN 1:10
KING JAMES (1611)	But let your communication be, Yea, yea; Nay, nay. . . .	Watch ye therefore, and pray always, that ye may be accounted worthy to escape all these things that shall come to pass. . . .	He was in the world, and the world was made by him, and the world knew him not.
AMERICAN STANDARD (1901)	But let your speech be, Yea, yea; Nay, nay. . . .	But watch ye at every season, making supplication, that ye may prevail to escape all these things that shall come to pass. . . .	He was in the world, and the world made through him, and the world know him not.
REVISED STANDARD (1946)	Let what you say be simply 'Yes,' or 'No'. . . .	Watch at all times, praying that you may have strength to escape all these things that will take place. . . .	He was in the world, and the world was made through him, yet the world knew him not.
NEW ENGLISH (1961)	Plain 'Yes' or 'No' is all you need to say. . . .	Be on the alert, praying at all times for strength to pass safely through all these imminent troubles. . . .	He was in the world; but the world, though it owed its being to him, did not recognize him.

95

ment published by Sheed and Ward in 1944) is:

Such is the peace thou hast enabled us to enjoy, so many wrongs have been righted for us through thy wisdom, that always and everywhere, most noble Felix, we are ready to acknowledge it with grateful hearts. But I must not weary thee with more of this; what we ask of thy courtesy is no more than a brief audience.

Elegant as this is, it suffers irremediably from one weakness: the archaic "thou" and "thee." No doubt God must be addressed in prayer as "Thou"; but it is not possible to imagine a public official nowadays listening without astonishment and amusement to a speaker beginning, "Such is the peace thou hast enabled us to enjoy"; and the Greek does not sound like that. (On the other hand, I think that Mgr. Knox's version, together with the Revised Standard Version, is superior to the new translation in one point of correctness: "always and everywhere" refers not to the improvements made by the government but to the gratitude felt by the Jews.)

The new translation leaves out words which, although customary in Greek, are needless in English. In the simple narrative style of the Gospels nearly every sentence is linked to its predecessor by a conjunction. Though usual in Greek narrative, this sounds silly in English, like an excited child telling a story. In the episode of the ungrateful lepers (Luke 17:11-19) seven out of eight sentences begin with "and." "And it came to pass . . . that he passed [!]. . . . And . . . there met him ten men . . . And they lifted up *their* voices. . . . And . . . he said unto them. . . . And it came to pass. . . ." and so on. These connectives are now eliminated, with the result that the narrative not only gains in speed and crispness but sounds more natural, more real.

The language of the Authorized Version is often terribly obscure. Anyone who has talked with devout Bible-readers ignorant of Greek and Hebrew will know what astounding traps they fall into, through misinterpreting its archaic and formal English. A friend of mine

once met a sectarian who found wartime tire rationing mentioned by the prophet Isaiah: "The Lord will take away the bravery of *their* tinkling ornaments *about their feet,* and *their* cauls, and *their* round tires like the moon. . . ." And an old lady of my acquaintance believes that "Sufficient unto the day *is* the evil thereof" means "to have exactly enough is to be miserable."

The new translation clears up many passages of the Bible by making the language simpler and more concrete. "God and mammon" was never clear to readers who did not know Aramaic, because "mammon" is the Aramaic word for "wealth" and must be an echo of the original speech of Jesus. Now it is replaced by what his hearers understood when he spoke the phrase "God and Money." "Publicans and sinners"—particularly confusing in Great Britain, where a publican is a man who keeps a pub—becomes "tax-gatherers and sinners," a phrase which is not only clearer but, to most of us, more graceful. "Scribes" are replaced by "lawyers"; "miracles" by "signs" (which is correct: the signs *revealed* or *manifested* Jesus' glory, John 2:11); the "candle . . . under a bushel" has become "the lamp under the meal-tub"; the "mote" and the "beam" (which have confused many people who did not know what a mote was and thought the beam might be a ray of light in the eye) have become "speck of sawdust" and "plank." "Charity" in Saint Paul's letter to the church at Corinth never was the kind of charity which we understand by the word, the giving of alms to the poor: it means pure nonsexual love; and in this translation, "love" it is.

Furthermore, the Greek form "Elias" is replaced by the Hebrew form, familiar to us from the Old Testament, "Elijah"; and "Christ" (the Greek word for "the Anointed") often by "Messiah." One might be tempted to replace the Greek form "Jesus" by the Aramaic or Hebrew original "Joshua"; but perhaps that would be going rather far. One of these changes, however, is rather a limitation than an expansion. Being British, the

translators have put the terms for money into what they believe to be British equivalents. When Judas complained about Mary of Bethany's waste of valuable perfume (not "ointment") poured over Jesus' feet, he said it could have been sold for "three hundred denarii." The King James Version makes this "three hundred pence," which is obviously wrong in today's values: what perfume could be bought for three hundred pennies a pound? The authors of the new translation Briticize it into "thirty pounds," with the literal version in a footnote. I should render it "three hundred pieces of silver," which is almost universally intelligible, and which reminds us of the price paid to Judas.

When Paul said, "It is better to marry than to burn," what did he mean? To burn in hell for the sin of sexual intercourse committed outside marriage? So I have heard it interpreted. The Greek word is *pyrousthai,* "to be aflame." Mgr. Knox gives, "better to marry than to feel the heat of passion"—which seems to exclude something of marital felicity. The new version says, "Better be married than burn with vain desire," which is perfectly clear, and correct. In the same way, important sentences which in earlier versions were inexplicably difficult are now intelligible. In the finest of his letters, Paul did not write, "Now we see through a glass, darkly": looking through glass is not seeing darkly, and anyhow the ancients did not use window glass until quite late. He wrote (in the new version), "Now we see only puzzling reflections in a mirror," a far more vivid and thoughtful image of mortal knowledge with all its imperfections.

Some may complain that this new translation lacks the poetry, even the magic, of the old. But the truth is that the traditional versions of the New Testament often overelaborated the original, made it sound nobler in English than it is in Greek. Most of the New Testament is very plain, even awkward, prose. In some places we can see that the writer is not even using his native tongue but translating from provincial Aramaic into vulgar Greek. There are some passages which are, even in the quiet Greek, poetic: the Blessings (why call them "Beatitudes"?), the Lord's Prayer, certain parables, certain ecstatic speeches of Jesus. These are rendered with grace, but without unnecessary ornamentation, in the new version. Outside of the biographies of Jesus, in the Letters (why "Epistles"?), there are many sections of more ambitious eloquence. These are rendered with suitable energy. The strange visions of the Book of Revelation suffer no diminution in the new rendering, and even gain, through its clarity, additional awe and power. This translation has started well and has passed some of the most exacting tests. Others are still to be confronted. We shall look forward with eager interest to see how the translators approach the loftier mysticism, the more complex narrative, and the richer poetry of the Hebrew Testament.

—GILBERT HIGHET

—To me, it sounds like Newspeak

I can't quite see why my good friend and HORIZON colleague Gilbert Highet, after approving the New English Bible's downgrading of "Christ" to "Messiah" and its elimination of "miracles" in favor of mere "signs," thinks its compilers would have been "going rather far" if they had also replaced "Jesus" by "Joshua." I don't think they would have been going too far at all. In fact, given the determination of these new brooms to fumigate Scripture and make a clean sweep of its accumulated errors and myths, it seems to me downright inconsistent of them not to expunge His traditional given name as well. But why "Joshua," which has an old-fashioned, faraway ring, too? If modernity, immediacy, and an approach to our own vernacular are the aim, why not assign to Him simply the generic handle of "Jones"?

If we are really to modernize the Bible, I say, let's do it in style. These apostles of the Electrolux approach to Holy Writ seem to me to lack the courage of their convictions: they don't follow through. They are either inhibited or, proficient as they no doubt are in ancient languages, don't really speak our own. Their spokesman proclaims in his introduction, "We have sought to avoid archaism, jargon, and all that is either stilted or slipshod." Great; but what do we get? In place of the obsolete reference in the King James Version of Luke to the "candle . . . under a bushel," an improved 1961 text reading "the lamp . . . under the meal-tub"—but what in heck is a meal-tub? In place of the encrusted parable in Matthew about sow-ing tares among the wheat, a streamlined story about sowing "darnel"—but what, pray (or rather, please) is darnel? King James's men in doublet and hose wrote of putting "new wine into old bottles"; now "bottles" have been updated, not to "flasks" or indeed "hip-flasks," but to "wine-skins." When did you refill your last wine-skin?

Just what language, in fact, do these new scribes actually speak? I fear the evidence is all too clear. For example, where Luke in King James writes (at 14:16), "A certain man made a great supper, and bade many. . . ." they spell this out into "A man was giving a big dinner party and had sent out many invitations." Where John formerly had Jesus begin, (in 8:14), "Though I bear record of myself. . . ." they improve this to, "My testimony is valid. . . ." Where in the older version Jesus said, "I am come in my Father's name. . . ." (John 5:43), we now have, "I have come accredited by my Father. . . ." And where Paul was once translated as writing simply (in I Corinthians 14:4), "He that prophesieth edifieth the church," this is now revised to, "It is prophecy that builds up a Christian community."

A duly accredited Christ arriving with valid testimony to attend high-level dinner parties for the sake of community-building—what have we here? I would say we have the jargon of official hand-out writers and lower-echelon bureaucrats. It has remained for the English to give Americans a Bible in Federalese.

And what a massive array of Englishmen, too, all with a tin ear! Representatives of the Church of England, the Church of Scotland, of two great Bible societies and of seven other denominations, including the English Methodists, Baptists, Congregationalists, Presbyterians, and Quakers, got together and set out to improve, for instance, on such a passage as Paul's, "When I was a child, I spake as a child, I understood as a child, I thought as a child. . . ." A little old-fashioned, a little hard to understand, maybe? They labored, and what did they come up with? This: "When I was a child, my speech, my outlook and my thoughts were all childish"—just as a Teachers' College student at work on a thesis on progressive kindergarten techniques might put it.

Next, these revisionists threaten us with a forward-looking, well-packaged and deflavorized redo of the Old Testament, too. On the basis of their precedent with the New, I can already imagine how it will read. They will, for instance, tackle the 23rd Psalm ("The Lord is my shepherd; I shall not want") and yield something like this:

The Almighty has taken me under his
   pastoral care; I won't be needy.
He encourages me to relax in unspoiled
   dairy country;
He steers me to out-of-the-way lakes.
He gives a lift to my spirit.
He leads me into highways of good
   citizenship so that I may identify
   with him.
Yes, though I drive through low-lying
   areas that may adversely affect
   my chances of survival,
I don't worry; for you are on my side;
Your guidance assures me with the
   feeling that I can implement it. . . .

—WILLIAM HARLAN HALE

97

Neo-realismo Revisited

One evening in 1945, when I had nothing better to do in the Maine town where I was spending the summer, I went to see *Wilson,* and after that I gave up Hollywood movies for five years. My repudiation was not convulsive; it was rather as if I had got a bad clam in a chowder, and while my reaction had been mild, my chemistry cautioned me to be wary of shellfish in the future.

Although I had eliminated Hollywood from my diet, my fare between 1945 and 1950 was sumptuous. I remember with admiration three semidocumentaries made in this country, far from the decorative but falsifying cosmetic of the West Coast studios: Louis de Rochemont's spy thriller, *The House on 92nd Street;* Robert Flaherty's *Louisiana Story* that told with articulate pictorial poetry of the discovery of oil in a Cajun bayou and the alterations thereafter in the lives of a simple Cajun family; and *The Quiet One,* Sidney Meyers's intelligent, merciful study of a maladjusted Negro boy. To name only a handful of the imported entertainments there were, from France, *Les Enfants du Paradis* (Marcel Carné's celebrated film) a cadenced romance played out against a nineteenth-century background; Jean Cocteau's adroit and phantasmal adaptation of *Beauty and the Beast; Symphonie Pastorale,* taken from André Gide's novella of a clergyman Pygmalion whose Galatea is a blind foundling. From England came David Lean's *Great Expectations,* as various as Dickens himself; Carol Reed's three notable creations, *The Third Man, The Fallen Idol,* and *Odd Man Out;* the Scotch frolic, *I Know Where I'm Going;* and Alec Guinness in that effervescent brew of monkeyshines, *The Lavender Hill Mob.*

By far the most impressive foreign pictures of that period of postwar delapidation and regenesis were those made by the Italian neo-realists who, refusing to dodge the issues by intoxicating themselves with pretty pipe dreams and resonant extravaganzas, looked unflinchingly at the way things really were —chaotic, ignoble, decayed, ragged at the edges. Through their films, mobs of unchildlike children roved in clothes too big for them: a precociously crafty and rapacious band of waifs worked with black-market hoodlums in Vittorio De Sica's *Shoeshine;* in Roberto Rossellini's memorable *Open City,* boys from a parochial school watched through a barbed-wire fence as their priest, a partisan, was shot by a German firing squad—the resignation in their dry eyes testifying to other monstrous things they had seen. De Sica's camera and Rossellini's, and those of Federico Fellini, Luigi Zampa, and Renato Castellani, picked up the empty Roman plazas, the murky courtyards, and the haunting fountains, the dazed faces of ordinary people on trolley cars, rangy cats walking cleverly over skylights, tides coming in, religious processions through country towns, dispirited prostitutes, and drunk GIs. Sick babies howled in wretched tenements where the blistered walls sweated; women pawned their sheets; old men sold their treasured books; hungry crowds looted bakeries; hope, when it was painfully born, was short-lived; and although the national persuasion to sing was irrepressible, arias from Puccini and Verdi were heard in counterpoint to the military music of the Fascisti. Nothing was certain and fear was quotidian.

These surgical and uncompromising probings of a society's ulcerated wounds were not accepted gratefully by Italian audiences, who wanted to wake from the nightmare of how life was into a dream of how it might be in a never-never land of sweetness and light and fun and games; they wanted cheesecake, not bitter rice. (The same cool reception has been accorded Satyajit Ray's Hindu trilogy in his own country, where moviegoers would prefer to identify for a moment with the rich and glittering rather than to look at the projections of their own downtrodden lives.) But despite the apathy of their countrymen, these radical directors continued to hold up to the public its flawed, twisted, and often heroic image. The products of their devotion included, besides *Shoeshine* and *Open City,* Rossellini's *Paisan,* a group of unrelated and unfinished episodes during the last years of the war as the Allies moved north from Sicily to the Po Valley; De Sica's profoundly disturbing *Bicycle Thief,* the tragedy of a laborer who, bereft of his bicycle, is bereft also of his job and who, in the hopeless search for the stolen machine, turns on his small son in a fury of frustration, introducing the boy to the pain of unkindness that is not deserved. *Umberto D.,* also the work of De Sica, is the portrait of a broke and friendless and homeless old man, marred by sentimentality but having nonetheless a great many dramatic details and photographic virtues. There were, somewhat later, Fellini's *I Vitelloni, Cabiria,* and his most famous, *La Strada,* a pathetic and Grand Guignol story of a free-lance strong man (played by Anthony Quinn) and a simple and simple-minded girl clown (Giulietta Masina) and their rural peregrinations from circuses to fairs to country weddings.

In recent years Italy has succumbed

In Roberto Rossellini's General Della Rovere *(1959), Vittorio De Sica portrays a petty crook who, in impersonating a patriot general, finally redeems himself.*

to money-making by capitalizing on sex and crime and melodrama, and the results have been largely tasteless; pin-up girls like Gina Lollobrigida and Sophia Loren have taken precedence over Anna Magnani, a vigorous actress who was not prettied up. Rossellini's scattered offerings have been commonplace, inert, uninstructive. But now he has returned to the irons of his original fire with *General Della Rovere*, and while I do not find this picture comparable to his sixteen-year-old masterpiece, *Open City*, it must, for its meanings and its movement, be taken seriously. The action takes place in 1943 and devolves about the metamorphosis of a picayune four-flusher into a decent man and a patriot. In Genoa, during the German occupation, Emanuele Bardone (suavely played by Vittorio De Sica) poses as a Colonel Grimaldi, an influential wirepuller who can effect the release of imprisoned partisans, and to this end he bilks their wives and kinsmen for the petty cash he needs to gamble and remain in good standing in brothels. His knavery is

handily discovered by Colonel Mueller (Hannes Messemer), the SS commandant in Genoa, and under pain of death Bardone is forced into a new and, this time, Machiavellian masquerade.

The Wehrmacht has learned that the anti-Fascist General Della Rovere is to land from a British submarine in the occupied zone, thence to make himself known to the leader of the underground, a man named Fabrizio, with whom he will plan the partisan strategy as the Germans retreat and the Allies advance. Through a miscarriage of orders the General is shot by the Nazis immediately on his getting to shore, and Mueller's hope to learn Fabrizio's identity is dashed. But only temporarily. By promising Bardone money and safe conduct to Switzerland, the German inveigles him into impersonating Della Rovere. Bardone is taken to a political prison, and there, for the other inmates, who know only the name of the General, he persuasively plays the role of military hero and unforgiving enemy of the Germans. The valedictories of men about to die,

scratched on the walls of the prison; the howls of the tortured, refusing to inform, that reverberate through the cell blocks; the awed respect of the prisoners for the man he is supposed to be, gradually begin to instill the amoral, apolitical, yellow, smalltime crook with character. And in the end, though he has the opportunity to expose Fabrizio to Mueller and to go free, he chooses to face a firing squad and thus end with grandeur a scrubby life.

General Della Rovere is overlong, and the pace, until the action in prison begins, is diffuse and wanting in tension. Then, however, it moves swiftly and passionately; the photography states rather than supposes, and the irrelevancies are more accentual than desultory. The ingredients are not novel: the well-tailored Teutonic hatchet men are by now as familiar as Dracula or shareholders in Murder, Inc., but they are still among the most unimpeachably detestable of cinematic villains. The understatement of the suffering of innocents, the camaraderie of men in jail,

Rossellini's Paisan *(1946)*

De Sica's The Bicycle Thief *(1949)*

De Sica's Umberto D. *(1952)*

Fellini's La Strada *(1954)*

the triumph of love of country over self-aggrandizement, the courageous acceptance of implacable destiny—all these basic elements of tragedy are skillfully and sometimes brilliantly employed. If I have reservations, I do so because I cannot help thinking of *Open City, The Bicycle Thief,* and *Shoeshine,* all of which I have recently seen again and with none of which can I find a single fault. Perhaps, though, this film is the beginning of the end of the doldrums for the Italian industry and we may see the renascence of the talents of these extraordinary dramatic commentators.

De Sica is, for my money, a much greater director than he is an actor. I acknowledge his finesse and the pliability of his handsome sorrowing face, his expressiveness of carriage, his immunity to histrionics; but the characters he elects to limn are either pathetic or elegiac, and I am impatient with his monotonous victimization or servility. But I am perpetually surprised by the daring ingenuity of his direction. In *Umberto D.* the old man, bereft of friends and family and a roof over his head, unable to find a home for his mongrel dog, is impelled to let it be killed rather than brutally starve to death; and for a breathless eternity, we watch all the cars of a long express train go by before we learn that the dog has not, after all, been crushed beneath the wheels. Again, in the episode "Therese" in *The Gold of Naples,* he keeps his camera on Silvana Mangano sobbing against a lamppost for a nearly intolerable length of time until he sends her back to the house of her bridegroom, an unhinged masochist who has married her, a whore, to do penance, by making himself socially unacceptable, for an earlier cruelty to a girl he had driven to suicide. De Sica's versatility shows at its most striking in the four vignettes that comprise *The Gold of Naples.* In two of them he exchanges his somber palette for a gaudy one and comes up with farce as noisy and funny as I have ever seen. Crockery crashes; eels writhe in the fists of madly

giggling children; priests collect money in baskets lowered from windows by dutiful parishioners who pause in their general screaming and singing to remember the needs of the Lord; a husband howls and flings himself into a mirror, giving himself an awful whack on the head, as he recalls, bellowing with remorse, that while his beloved wife was dying he was eating a pizza. The inspired comedian Toto does a lunatic dance of joy on a balcony when he at last manages to evict his guest of ten years, a gangster who had moved in with Toto and his hapless family after the death of his wife. This squatter for a decade had complained about the food and about the way the unwilling hostess had laundered his collars, and since the press of business in the underworld allowed him no leisure time, had delegated his host to go daily to the grave of the deceased with flowers and prayers for her immortal soul.

Federico Fellini, once a protégé of Rossellini and now eminent in his own right, has said in an interview with Gideon Bachmann (*Film: Book 1, The Audience and the Filmmaker,* edited by Robert Hughes, Grove Press Inc.): "It is completely useless to prepare a statement for a crowd, or make a film with a message for everyone. I don't believe in talking to a crowd. Because what is a crowd? It is a collection of many individuals, each with his own reality. That is also the reason why my pictures never end. . . . when you show a true problem and then resolve it, the spectator is beguiled into feeling that the problems in his own life, too, will solve themselves, and he can stop working on them for himself." This is a solemn creed, and it limits the uses of fiction; it eliminates the impossible, the castle in Spain, and the pot of gold at the end of the rainbow. Still, it is a creed of integrity, and it admits of the effect of accidents upon essences: the catalyst of circumstance transforms Bardone, as, at some time in our lives, it transforms us all, for better or worse. —JEAN STAFFORD

ADVERTISING

Today's Temple of Talent

Leaf through a current magazine, or listen long enough to your television set, and sooner or later your attention will be brought up sharply by a sentence so artfully written or a picture so cunningly composed that it will defy your best efforts to pass it by. You are not likely to be elated by the experience, because you will be paying unwilling heed to some message about a deodorant, a hair tonic, a motor oil, or the like. This may even lead you to deny that the sentence was indeed artful, or the picture cunning.

But they were. More than that—and it is no pleasant thing to be forced to admit it—the level of talent on display is far above the level currently being displayed in the popular arts. There has been, for example, a television commercial for Maxwell House coffee that begins with nothing more than the first bubble of boiling water in a percolator and builds upon that an arresting rythmic melody that accelerates in tempo and complexity as the boiling increases —a catchy, jumpy melody that you would like to hear again. I can't remember anything this skillful in, say, *Tenderloin*, or indeed in any musical comedy since—let me see—"Fugue for Tinhorns" in *Guys & Dolls*. And then there may be those who remember another television commercial, for Johnson & Johnson, some time ago. They will have to remember it, because I can't describe it. It was constructed around multiple-exposure motion-picture photography and a few basic sounds. The commercial vanished rather quickly, so perhaps it failed to sell Band-Aids, but it was bolder and more arresting than anything I have seen in a motion-picture theater over the last ten years. It is more difficult to single out the praiseworthy prose, since in prose the meaning and the style

are interwoven, and a distaste for the one taints any attempt to look closely at the other. But it certainly is possible to detect in the better advertisements a clarity and a crispness that I don't often find in the volumes that the Book-of-the-Month Club shovels under my door.

Advertising is, after all, the wedding of artistic talent to commercial drive, brought about by the provision of a substantial dowry. I have a good deal of respect for artistic talent, and I enjoy what it can produce when it is left to go about its business—the novel, the poem, the song, and the play. On the other hand, I have always been puzzled by the contrast between the talent and the person in whom it is housed. I have long since learned never to seek out an acquaintance with a writer whose novels I deeply admire. Those novels may very well be wise, perceptive, and deeply moving; the author is likely to be fumbling, obtuse, and dubiously capable of crossing a busy street without aid. And the novelist is ordinarily a man of enormous cultivation compared with the musician and the painter.

Obviously I am mistaken. Their works prove to me that I am mistaken, for I can not bring myself to believe that a stupid man can write a wise book—at least, not very often. What puts me off, I suspect, is not a lack of ability but a lack of vitality. The artist, by and large, cuts a paltry figure in his social life because the good Lord, who gave him an abundance of talent, balanced the books by withholding his share of drive and of energy. He comments on life, but he takes only a small part in it. James Thurber once pointed out that a poet would rather leap into print with his ladylove than into bed with her.

It may be that the principal charge

to be brought against advertising is that from a shallow reservoir of real talent it skims off exactly those men and women who do manage to enjoy a certain vitality along with their precious abilities. The copy writer must battle for his prose; battle every day with the art director, the account executive, the client, and the competing copy writer. It is not the sort of occupation that the diffident man will choose, or will tolerate for long. And although he may be well aware that what he actually sets down on paper is beneath his dignity, he is paid well for it and is thus kept (as Herman Hickman once said in an entirely different connection) sullen but not mutinous.

It seems reasonable to believe that this accounts for the fact that the lively arts have become consistently less lively during the course of the last thirty or forty years. The men and women with drive and spirit have been seduced by an industry that gives them ample scope for exercising their talents, pays them well for the job, and asks only that they forebear to look too closely at the finished product.

There is some risk that I may be misunderstood, so let me make it clear that I would far rather read a well-meant second-rate novel than the most skillfully articulated glob of advertising copy, and I would rather see a moderately entertaining musical comedy than a well-turned commercial. But the first-rate novel and the great musical don't come our way as often as they once did, and I think we can attribute our deprivation to the flourishing advertising industry. That's the way it is working out, and perhaps the best recourse is to cultivate a taste for advertising so that we can appreciate the style and ignore the content. —STEPHEN WHITE

Human Beings and Substitutes

A disconcerting experience at the theater is the sensation of inadequate response. To be present when matters of urgency are examined, and to know oneself uninvolved, produces a spiritual scruffiness akin to the guilt induced by moral evasion. In our day there are dramatists of high resolution and impressive power—Tennessee Williams is the most notable one in this country, as John Osborne is in England—who send me home in the late evening dispirited and estranged from whatever is creative in my own make-up.

Although Williams and Osborne are above all else plausible writers, and each has a bird dog's instinct for the presently relevant theme, what they lack is the love for individual personality that is the fever of true storytellers. In its stead they display a preoccupation with general symptoms that is the bias of therapists. They automate fashionable predicaments, but they do it so cleverly—and I will believe honorably—that one's senses cannot tell the human surrogates from God's creatures. But a kind of animal instinct rejects what schooled eyes and ears may be willing to accept; therefore one slopes along home in a yellow mood, depressed because such excellent simulacra did not pass the tests by which every species recognizes its own.

The dramatist's problem of securing an adequate response was brought into focus for me by seeing recently, on successive evenings, performances of Tennessee Williams's *Period of Adjustment* and Shelagh Delaney's *A Taste of Honey*. Both plays are skillfully written in the vernacular of present-day concerns; both are admirably produced and performed. Mr. Williams calls his work a "serious comedy"; Miss Delaney offers

no label, but hers could fairly be called a witty tragedy. It comes to much the same thing; but *Period of Adjustment* dulls the spirit, and *A Taste of Honey* puts new shine on the human race.

Subject matter is not at issue. Mr. Williams, to be sure, has changed his mask without making any notable shift in his fixed gaze: he is concerned, as in his succession of violent tragedies, with the guilt of impotence, the horror of castration, and the danger of the devouring female. But these are valid concerns—symbolically, they certainly are—and in any case Miss Delaney's material is scarcely more gladsome. She offers a chronicle of life in a Lancashire slum wherein a girl is deserted by her trampish mother, made pregnant by a Negro sailor on leave, befriended by a homosexual art student, and last seen crouched alone in her tenement flat, crooning to herself a nursery rhyme and enduring the first spasms of labor. It sounds stubbornly sordid when you omit the humanity of these people, but that is precisely what Miss Delaney does not omit. Indeed, it is her reason for writing.

Tennessee Williams's reason for writing is not so quickly stated and in the end must be more inferred than proved. One thing seems certain, though; he is driven from within, not attracted from without. At the time when he was working on *Period of Adjustment* he had this to say: "My back is to the wall and has been to the wall for so long that the pressure of my back on the wall has started to crumble the plaster that covers the bricks and mortar." A man who senses himself to be in that extreme situation must necessarily be intent on extricating himself; and, in fact, a little later in the same article, written for the New

York *Times*, Mr. Williams confesses: "At the age of fourteen I discovered writing as an escape from a world of reality in which I felt acutely uncomfortable."

Speculation on that statement would lead me into the area of art as therapy, where debate is savage and endless, and I want to stay with *Period of Adjustment*. It concerns two couples who, at the beginning of the play, find themselves mentally and physically estranged and who, at the final curtain, are tumbling into their respective beds with the happiest anticipations. Bravo! And good for them. But we, unhappily, have been obliged to stand by for two hours while they made their trek through the psychological rain forest, and a melancholy session I, at least, found it to be.

Conformity is depressing, and these Williams characters are worse than conformist—they are composites. They are so, probably not by design, but as the inevitable result of Mr. Williams's method. Standing there with his back crumbling the plaster, he knows himself beset by harpies; and it seems to him that the way to make these evil birds significant is to show that he is no special victim, that in fact they will devour the most unremarkable flesh. That bespeaks a kind of modesty and a decent concern for others; it may even be true. But I am persuaded that it leads Mr. Williams to work with clay so commonplace that the breath will never enter. He seems to derive his people as Mr. Gallup derives his opinions—by averages that approach homogeneity. The characters in *Period of Adjustment* are real not by intuition but by definition: they are compiled from all the television commercials, suburban sociologies, Norman Rockwell magazine covers, and

master-of-ceremonies jokes that have ever passed before Mr. Williams's suffering eyes and ears. The results are not genuine people; they are genuine statistics—and statistics burdened with a characteristic Williams tic. The tic is something we are expected to recognize and sympathize with; but neuroses do not look plausible in manikins, and sympathy wavers and turns rancid when its object is a generalization. So one retreats from this "serious comedy," baffled and dismayed by the insipidity of suffering humanity. Relief comes when you see that though the suffering may be genuine, the humanity in this instance is only an advertising dummy.

Miss Delaney was just nineteen when she wrote *A Taste of Honey,* and she naturally went about the job in a much simpler way. She has said that she was prodded to write by a dissatisfaction with the way people of her world were portrayed in plays she saw while working as a theater usher: "The North Country people usually are not shown as they are, for in actual fact they are very alive and cynical. I write as people talk." That is as quiet—and as bold—a boast as a writer can well make, and Miss Delaney quietly lives up to it.

Jo Smith, the girl, is a vulnerable little bitch with a sharp tongue and a ready heart, both engendered by loneliness. Helen, her mother, is an overblown peony, with a mind as errant as a kite let loose and appetites as sharp as a fox's. Geoffrey, a sort of Dutch aunt to Jo, saves his dignity from the traps of pettiness and a tendency to flounce by a real generosity of concern.

One falls quickly, almost eagerly, into intimacy with these people because they possess that most engaging virtue of un-

In Shelagh Delaney's A Taste of Honey *(above) Joan Plowright portrays a waif, pregnant and abandoned; Andrew Ray plays a motherly male who cares for her. In contrast to these oddly affecting people, Tennessee Williams presents in* Period of Adjustment *two stereotyped married couples. Three of his principals are Barbara Baxley, James Daly, and Robert Webber (below).*

derstanding themselves. Helen, in brief lapses from avid sensuality, grimaces sourly at the comedy of her aging susceptibility; Jo is rarely quite free of a self-mockery induced by admitting that the very real misery of being a waif is considerably softened in her case by the virtuosity with which she rings changes on the role. And Geoffrey's too fragile outburst of masculine aggression not only defines for us his essential femininity, as no amount of attenuated extravagance could do it, but confirms himself to himself. He becomes a denser,

a more substantial, figure after one flaccid embrace has shown him pitilessly what way he will never go.

When these three defiant egos cross one another, wit flashes, the sensibilities bleed, allegiances are sprained. It is a battle for communication, a struggle for security, a search for purpose; and it is not resolved—except for the resolution that it will go on. When the curtain falls on *A Taste of Honey,* Jo and Helen and Geoffrey are licking their paws and planning their next sorties on life; when it falls on *Period of Adjustment,* the characters are stacked in the wings, ready for the next demonstration.

A final note: it is being said that Joan Plowright makes a personal triumph of *A Taste of Honey.* So she does, in the sense that she turns Jo into a miracle of meager vitality. Her gestures are half woman, half don't-give-a-damn; she can crow like a young rooster, and she has a way of smirking when hurt that I doubt I shall ever forget. But it is not a triumph in the sour sense that she outclasses her company. Angela Lansbury's earth mother turned barmaid and weekend wife is brilliantly discriminating where she could be just blowzily smothering; and Andrew Ray has probably made American theater history with his unabashed, unsentimental portrayal of Geoffrey; his gentle, waspish boy is the first stage homosexual I have seen who was not an invitation to guffaws or pious horror. The New York production was directed by Tony Richardson and George Devine after the pattern established in London by Joan Littlewood. A jazz quartet in the background underscores the syncopated realism of Miss Delaney's tribute to the people she knows. —ROBERT HATCH

103

BY JOHN CANADAY

GARGOYLES FOR THE MACHINE AGE

Odd materials go into a sculpture of odder shapes

Contemporary sculptors, who for some reason are about ten times as imaginative as contemporary painters, are having a wonderful time these days concocting a breed of monsters that can either scare the daylights out of you or tickle your ribs, depending on the nature of your sensibility to a form of art that combines wit with tentative forays into regions of darkness peculiar to the twentieth century. Although scrap metal is a favorite material of these sculptors, and the welding gun their most necessary tool, they have a lot in common with the medieval stone carvers whose cathedral gargoyles were the offspring of a similarly mixed but high-spirited marriage between the humorous and the sinister that produced its natural hybrid, the grotesque.

Fear of hell on one hand and rollicking gusto for life on the other produced the medieval gargoyles. Today we have ceased to believe in hell, and gusto is in short supply. But neo-gargoyle sculpture (the phrase is the invention of a colleague, Stuart Preston) can be interpreted as the expression of contemporary fears plus a contemporary zest for experiment and speculation.

A typical new gargoyle may be composed of such detritus of the machine age as discarded gears, pipes, metal meshes, screens and gratings, bits of iron or steel plate, and any of the thousands of discs, perforated plates, or oddly shaped and punctured units that have been stamped out to serve a special purpose yet become aesthetic curiosa when accepted out of context as objects with an independent existence. Cinders and slag are good, too, with their horrendous textures and bizarre shapes. Even the sculptors who work with new material like to gash it, melt it, score it, pit it, and crumple it into proper condition.

All art being a process of the transformation of material into expression, the term junk sculpture need be no more derogatory than the term oil painting. Junk sculpture becomes art when it meets the terms that make other forms of sculpture "good" or "bad" art. By one general definition, classical in implication, art is the distillation of order and meaning from the chaotic material of human experience. By direct analogy, if the junk sculptor can take the chaotic detritus of our machine age and reassemble

TEXT CONTINUED ON PAGE 113

Frog Eating a Lizard (*nineteen inches high*) *is the work of a young Englishman, Eduardo Paolozzi. After he had built up his ferocious frog of clay and bits of junk, the whole thing was cast in bronze.*

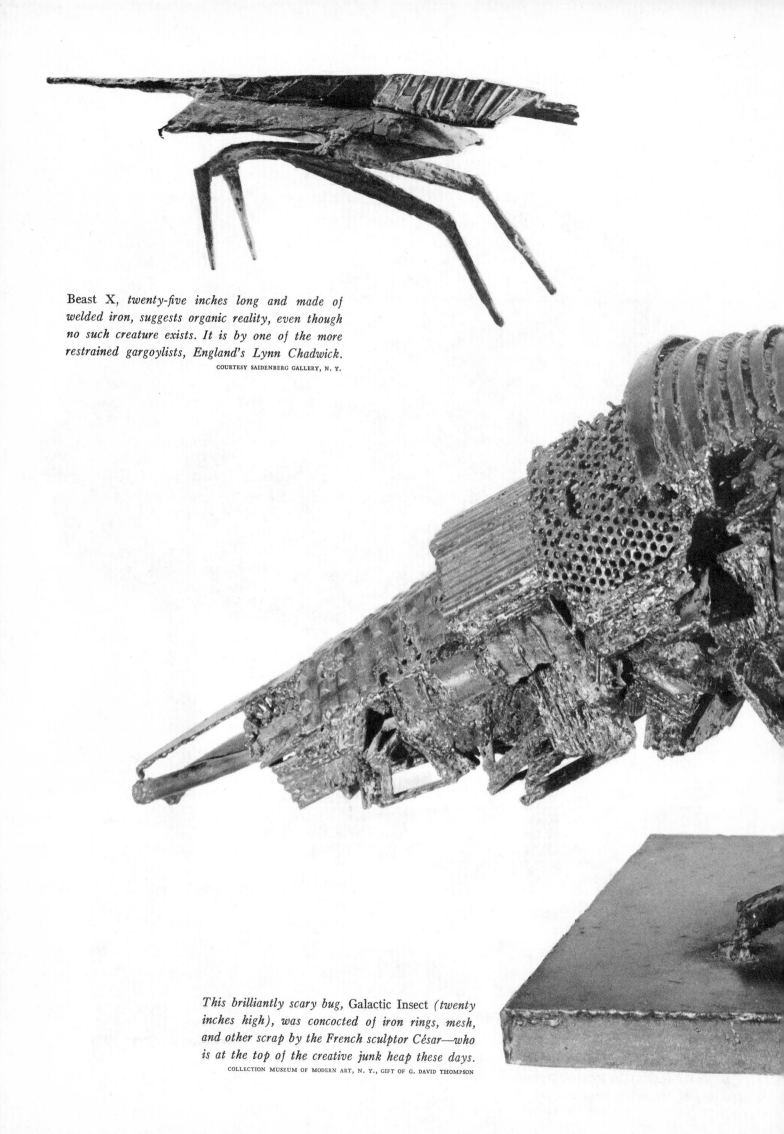

Beast X, *twenty-five inches long and made of welded iron, suggests organic reality, even though no such creature exists. It is by one of the more restrained gargoylists, England's Lynn Chadwick.*

This brilliantly scary bug, Galactic Insect (twenty inches high), was concocted of iron rings, mesh, and other scrap by the French sculptor César—who is at the top of the creative junk heap these days.

Robert Müller's Stele for a Termite *is a monstrously engaging memorial of welded scrap iron (thirty-five inches high). Müller, a Swiss, is well known in Europe and will soon have his first New York show.*

Another of Müller's monumental apparitions looks like a crouching beast, but he calls it The Roasting Spit. About forty-three inches long, it was forged out of sheet-iron plates he found in dumps.

Knight of Darkness *is a thirty-six-inch figure in slag and clinkers by Jean Dubuffet. Better known as a painter, he has often been called the most important artist to emerge in France since the war.*

COLLECTION MR. AND MRS. ALBERT A. LIST, N. Y.

Seared, scarred, and almost molten-looking, Elisabeth Frink's bronze Bird (seventeen inches high) could be either a recollection of the recent past or a prophetic vision. The artist is an English newcomer.

COURTESY BERTHA SCHAEFER GALLERY, N. Y.

César's cast-iron Winged Figure (fifty-six inches long) suggests a ruined fusion of bird, Greek Victory, and airplane—or natural history, classical art, and technology sharing a universal holocaust.

COLLECTION MR. AND MRS. RICHARD K. WEIL, ST. LOUIS

*Sinisterly car-conscious, the young American John
Chamberlain uses materials salvaged from wrecks for
constructions like Wildroot (sixty-six inches high).*

TEXT CONTINUED FROM PAGE 104

it into forms that have a satisfactory relationship to one another as an aesthetic whole, then he has indeed created a legitimate work of art from material—both physical and ideological—afforded only by our time.

The classical premises of purity and order, however, are dubious ones for the defense of junk sculpture. But turn the junk sculptor loose on romantic premises and he has it made. The job of the romantic is not to purify but to intensify, not to resolve but to stimulate, not so much to answer as to ask, and when he does answer, to answer by implication rather than by definition. Suggestion, free association, experiment, revolt, even fortuitous accident, are his meat. And the romantic artist has always had an interest in the exploration of decay that makes one wonder why it took him so long to discover the junk heap as his happiest hunting ground.

The fascination held by ruined machinery for the sculptor today may have its parallel once removed in the fascination held by ruined architecture for his nineteenth-century counterpart. His gargoyles suggest mangled and intermingled mutations of men, birds, beasts, and machines. His ruins are not reminders of the past, crumbling in the weather and devoured by foliage like the ones adored a hundred years ago, but are deformed as if prophetically by the aberrations of science that may yet produce the ultimate holocaust. This is the hell that we can conceive of today, and some of the gargoyles seem already to have approached close enough to its terrible boundaries to have been broken, seared, and fused into forms such as men have never seen, but might some day see too much of.

But of course it may not happen, and in the meanwhile man is up to an old trick of mental self-preservation: a large element of fun is introduced into fearful conjectures. This accounts for the double-barreled appeal of the new gargoyles. Things are pretty bad, they imply, and may get worse. But in the meanwhile this shaky crust we are walking on has an interesting bounce to it.

John Canaday is art editor of the New York Times *and author of* Mainstreams of Modern Art.

113

Voltaire at thirty-eight

By HAROLD NICOLSON

"He taught us to be free"

Although he was an absolutist, not especially reasonable, and anything but a revolutionary, Voltaire fought absolutism, embodied the Age of Reason, and made the Revolution inevitable

The supreme intellectual, as distinct from emotional, influence of the eighteenth century was that exercised by Voltaire. He was born in 1694 and died in 1778 at the age of eighty-four. It' was he who taught three generations that superstition was ridiculous, sentiment absurd, fanaticism unintelligent, and oppression infamous. He was a brilliant satirist rather than a constructive or even logical philosopher. His plays, his epic, and his occasional verse were much admired by his contemporaries; his historical writings remain perfect models of French prose; his short stories, although not fully appreciated at the time, had a lasting influence; his conversation was witty and his vast correspondence a monument of lucidity and almost of candor; his open quarrels with the eminent became the talk of Europe; and, although his literary taste was questionable, his political and philosophic apothegms changed the thinking habits of the civilized world.

He was the inventor of that critical habit of thought which sapped faith in the established system, which deprived the upper class of its self-confidence, and which became one of the causes of the French Revolution. Thus when in 1791 the Revolution had triumphed, the National Assembly decreed that his coffin should be removed from the distant village in which he had

been buried and transported in state to the Panthéon in Paris. Escorted by the National Guard, it rumbled through the streets of Paris in a hearse designed by the painter David and bearing the inscription, "He taught us. to be free." The funeral procession was followed by a hundred thousand mourners, and the windows, the balconies, and the sidewalks were packed with further thousands gathered to acclaim its passage. The hearse halted outside the Opéra, outside the Palace of the Tuileries, and stopped at the house on the Quai des Théatins (thenceforward and to this day to be known as the Quai Voltaire) where he had died. It was there that the two daughters of Calas, whom he had defended against oppression, stepped forward and kissed the coffin. The crowds cheered and sobbed. Then on to the Comédie Francaise, where a huge placard carried the words, "He wrote *Oedipe* at seventeen"; to the Théâtre Français, where another placard proclaimed, "He wrote *Irène* at eighty-four." At last the vast procession reached the Panthéon and the coffin was carried to its vault.

Twenty-three years later, when the Bourbons were restored to the throne, the reactionaries had his bones, together with those of Jean Jacques Rousseau, exhumed from the Panthéon and cast into a pit outside the city, where they were consumed by quick-

lime. This posthumous revenge was not discovered until 1864, when the coffin, on being opened, was found to be empty. It at least proved that the adherents of the old regime regarded him and Rousseau as their bitterest enemies.

He was not, as has been said, a profound thinker. He taught men to question every legend, every conventional idea transmitted to them by their parents, and to believe nothing that could not be confirmed by the evidence of the senses. He exposed shams. Since the whole structure of society at the outset of the eighteenth century was founded on make-believe, the blast of his irony, the flame of his sarcasm had a withering effect. He was one of the most potent destructive writers that have ever lived; but he was not constructive.

Although it is correct to acclaim him as a great champion of the freedom of thought and expression, although he was assuredly the unflagging and unflinching opponent of oppression, whether political or religious, it would be an error to describe him as a revolutionary. He was not a political scientist, and if he had any ideal of human government, it was the Platonic ideal of the philosopher king, assisted by an elite of cultivated nobles. He did not believe that all men were created equal, nor did he possess any real conception of liberty as a balance of rights and duties guaranteed by an impartial and known system of laws. He was an absolutist, even as Rousseau was an absolutist; but whereas Rousseau desired the dictatorship of the proletariat, Voltaire desired the dictatorship of kings.

Thus, whereas he was constantly extolling freedom of thought and expression as secured in England, he felt that the central government had every right to prosecute those who openly attacked them. He refused to accept, or even to recognize, Montesquieu's distinction between despotism and constitutional monarchy. The very idea of a limited central authority was to him abhorrent. "No government," he wrote, "can be in any manner effective unless it possesses absolute power." He had no sympathy whatsoever for the common man. "Once the populace begins to reason," he wrote to Frederick the Great, "then everything is lost. I abominate the idea of government by the masses." One of his most frequent mottoes was a line from Racine: *Que Rome soit toujours libre et César tout-puissant.*

That it never occurred to him that this was in itself an untenable paradox shows that his political thought was immature and muddled. He looked to his benevolent and all-powerful monarch, his philosopher king, to introduce practical reforms. He was not blind to the fact that the whole theory and system of the *ancien régime* was out of date. He was in favor of the most drastic administrative reforms, such as more equitable taxation, the abolition of arbitrary arrest and secret trials, the suppression of the feudal privileges of the aristocracy, the elimination of all internal customs barriers, and the promulgation of a new penal code by which both torture and the death penalty should be abolished. There were times even when he dimly realized that true liberty meant the absolute equality of all citizens under the law. "To be free," he wrote, "implies being subject to law alone. The English love their law in the same way as a father loves his children, because they created it themselves, or are at least under the impression that they created it."

He regarded nationalism, even patriotism, as emotions unworthy of the rational man. Whereas Montesquieu was tenderly patriotic and Rousseau, when it suited him, could sob aloud when he thought of his native Geneva, Voltaire had no special feelings for France. He thought it most "unreasonable" for nationalists, such as the patri-

ots of Poland or the American plantations, to rebel against the established government. He would have agreed with Goethe that nationalism is the sign of a low standard of culture. He would have regarded himself, not so much as a French subject, but as a good European, even as a citizen of the world. And we must admit that patriotism, for all its inspiration and splendor, is an emotional rather than intellectual concept.

A similar lack of logic can be observed in his attitude towards religion. He detested any form of religious fanaticism or what he called "enthusiasm." It was not merely that he denied the claims of the Pope to be spiritual and even temporal arbiter of the universe, and that he assailed all persecution on the part of the ecclesiastical or state authorities of those who differed from them in their form of belief; it was also that he detested any form of religious intolerance, whether Catholic, Protestant, or Presbyterian. He did not mind the Jesuits so much, since they were subtle, cultured, and believed to some extent in the divine right of kings. What he loathed were the Jansenists, "the Calvinists of Catholicism," who taught the doctrine of original sin, of salvation through Grace, and who believed, as did the Puritans of New England, that only the "elect" would be saved, whereas the rest of humanity was destined for eternal damnation. He suspected the Jansenists of being at heart "sour republicans," and in his shocking but widely read lampoon on Joan of Arc he describes a typical Jansenist as "the slave of destiny, the lost child of Grace."

He certainly admitted the social value of some organized religion and remarked sarcastically that if the most violent atheist "had five or six hundred peasants to manage he would certainly inculcate into them the doctrine of a God dispensing punishments and rewards." On his estate at Ferney he pulled down the village church, since it obstructed his view, but he obtained permission from the Bishop to build a new one in its place and inscribed over the portal the words *Deo erexit Voltaire.* He even on Easter Sunday attended mass in this church and insisted on preaching a sermon from the pulpit. On his deathbed he agreed to receive the Sacraments and was buried according to the rites of the Church.

Such inconsistencies render it hard for us to determine whether Voltaire was merely anticlerical, or whether he denied the fundamental truths of revealed religion. He

would have described himself as a deist. He contended that the fact that some men are possessed of better minds than others, and that the firmament moves and circles with intricate regularity, implies that there must exist a "supreme geometrician" who ordains and orders such things. It is absurd to assert that there is no such thing as "superior intelligence" or that all men are born with equal capacities. "Certainly," he writes, "there exists a difference between the ideas of Newton and the droppings of a mule." He does not pretend to define the nature or location of his "supreme geometrician." "All I can do," he asserts, "is to worship him." The assumption is that the geometrician is all-powerful and benevolent. "From an all-perfect being," says Voltaire, "evil cannot result."

It is probable that Voltaire would all his life have maintained this comfortable balance between conformity, deism, and a hatred of intolerance and persecution had it not been for the shock given to his conscience by the Lisbon earthquake of November 1, 1755. The report, as it first reached him, was that fifteen thousand men, women, and children had, within the space of six minutes, been crushed beneath the bells and towers of Lisbon's churches, which were packed for divine service on All Saints' Day. The disaster of Lisbon produced on the minds of that generation an effect as morally and mentally disturbing as the destruction of Hiroshima has produced on ours. How can God, they questioned, really be an all-powerful and benevolent deity if He can murder thousands of innocent humans at the moment that they are gathered together to do Him worship?

Several different answers were returned to this distressing question. It was not denied that out of a population of 275,000 some 10,000 to 15,000 lost their lives; that damage to the extent of twelve million pounds had been caused to the city; that thirty churches had been destroyed either by the earthquake itself or by the ensuing fire and tidal wave; and that valuable libraries and muniments had perished, including pictures by Titian, Correggio, and Rubens. How was this ferocious act of God to be explained? The Portuguese themselves were convinced that the disaster was an act of divine vengeance upon a sinful world. But if so, then why should so many priests and nuns, as well as so many sacred images, have been obliterated by the catastrophe and so many heretics, evil persons, and objects of idolatry have been spared? The Jesuits also contended that the earthquake was not due, as some unbelievers had the audacity to aver, to natural causes, but was an overt demonstration of the wrath of God. The Jansenist Laurent Etienne Rondet wrote a whole book to prove that the disaster was a divine comment on the iniquity of the Inquisition and the Jesuits. The Protestants of London argued that it must be ascribed to God's disapproval of the Portuguese in general, and Lisbon in particular, for their addiction to abominable papal practices and their avowed worship of the Mother of God. It was even suggested that the Saints had begged God to choose their own particular festival as the date for his demonstration.

Voltaire was shaken by the event out of his facile optimism, his confidence in the doctrine that all is best in the best possible of worlds, his adherence to the theodicy of Leibnitz, his egoistic complacency. His poem on *The Disaster of Lisbon* is one of the most sincere that he ever wrote. How can we believe this frightful holocaust was planned and desired by a benevolent God?

Quel crime, quelle faute ont commis ces enfants
Sur le sein maternel écrasés et sanglants?

If God had in fact desired to inflict punishment on the Portuguese, could He not have chosen a less atrocious method? Only He can explain His actions, but He refuses to do so, leaving His children as "bewildered atoms in a mass of mud." It was then that Voltaire first conceived the idea of his excellent story *Candide*, which is in effect a satire on the whole optimistic school. Candide, who had been taught by the philosopher Pangloss to believe in the loving-kindness of God and the perfectibility of man, is exposed to a series of frightful misfortunes and finds that throughout the world, with the solitary exception of the legendary country of Eldorado, man is cruel, greedy, and inconceivably stupid. He is at Lisbon at the time of the earthquake and exclaims in agony, "If this be indeed the best of all possible worlds, then what must the other worlds be like?" He meets the philosopher Martin who takes a more realistic view of this world and the next. Candide asks him whether men have always been as wicked, cruel, hypocritical, perfidious, greedy, and stupid as they seem today. The following dialogue ensues: " 'Do you believe,' said Martin, 'that hawks

have always wanted to devour pigeons?' 'Certainly,' answered Candide. 'Well,' replied Martin, 'if hawks have always had the same character, how do you expect men to alter theirs?' 'Oh,' explained Candide, 'there is a great difference between hawks and men, since the latter possess free will. . . .' Arguing in this manner they reached Bordeaux."

The Lisbon earthquake taught Candide to reject the theories of his old teacher Pangloss and to adopt the agnostic stoicism of Martin. "You should work," says the latter, "and not waste time in speculation: this is the only way to render life endurable." Candide sighs deeply and accepts this doctrine. The story ends with the famous *"mais il faut cultiver notre jardin."*

After the Lisbon earthquake Voltaire ceased to be so certain about his deism, so confident in the great Geometrician, and lapsed into a vague form of agnosticism, arguing that since we could never expect in this world to understand the purposes of Providence, we must avoid abstract speculation, content ourselves with daily tasks, and cling to hope. "Why do we exist?" he wrote. "Why is anything anything?"

If we are to understand the movement of thought in the eighteenth century, it is thus necessary to be aware of the deep and wide repercussions produced by the Lisbon earthquake throughout Europe and beyond. Goethe, who was but six years old at the time, remembered how "the demon of fright" then spread across the world. Everybody explained this act of God as a justification of their own prejudices. Rousseau took it as a warning to mankind that it was highly dangerous to live in crowded cities. Warburton, in his Fast-Day sermon, argued that the earthquake was a benevolent warning to all mankind and "displayed God's glory in its fairest colours." John Wesley, who can have known nothing of what had really occurred in those Lisbon churches and along the harbor wharves, asserted that God's warning had been directed, "not to the small vulgar, but the great—to the learned, rich, and honourable heathens commonly called Christians." If Wesley were correct in this deduction, then why was it the "small vulgar" among the Portuguese people who had suffered the greatest casualties? Certainly the news of the earthquake aroused a mood of self-examination and repentance throughout the world. "Between the French and the Earthquake," wrote Horace Walpole to

Henry Conway, "you have no notion how good we are grown; nobody makes a suit now but of sackcloth turned up with ashes."

And it is a fact that masquerades, which until then had been the rage of London, were abandoned forever.

The life and character of Voltaire is a fascinating study and one which amply repays the labor involved. The strange thing is that for all his literary activity (he would rise at dawn and start dictating to a secretary in the very act of clambering out of bed) he found time to amass a huge personal fortune. He was himself reticent about his money-making methods, and in *Candide* he asserts that the art of making money consists in "having been born lucky." It seems however that as a young man he speculated on army contracts and thereafter prospered as a moneylender, providing cash advances to impoverished nobles at a high rate of interest. He was stingy in small ways, being mean about tips and candles. Until he purchased the estate of Ferney, he lived most of the time at the expense of other people, accumulating a fortune meanwhile which rendered him, by modern standards, a multimillionaire. No wonder that Rousseau in his hermitage or Diderot in his attic should have looked on Voltaire as different from themselves.

He was born in Paris on November 21, 1694, the son of Maître Arouet, who was highly respected in legal circles and acted as solicitor to the Saint-Simon family as well as to the ageless courtesan Ninon de l'Enclos. He was educated at Louis-le-Grand but refused, much to his father's fury, to study for the bar. At the age of nineteen he was attached to the staff of the Marquis de Châteauneuf, ambassador to the States-General. At the Hague he had a passionate love affair with Olympe Dunoyer, which caused such scandal that he was sent back to Paris in disgrace and for a short period sought to allay his father's displeasure by entering a lawyer's office. At the age of twenty he attracted the attention of the Marquis de Saint-Ange, who invited him to stay at the Château de Saint-Ange and instructed him in the manners of the court while telling much about the grandeur and pettiness of Versailles in the time of the *roi soleil*. He was always a brilliant talker, and his malicious sallies and epigrams gave him a welcome in the salons of Paris. He was even admitted into the charmed circle of the Duchesse du Maine at Sceaux. His

This old German version of the Lisbon disaster shows everything happening at once—earthquake, fire, and tidal waves—although these events actually followed each other.

facility for composing monkeyish little lampoons upon the great soon earned him the repute of being a dangerous young man. On May 16, 1717, at the age of twenty-two, he was suddenly sent, under a *lettre de cachet,* to prison at the Bastille. He was charged with being the author of an epigram which had in fact been written by someone else. The injustice of this sentence filled him with a lasting hatred of arbitrary arrest and instilled into him the principle that nobody should be convicted without open trial and on the ground that he had broken some known and published law. So disgusted was he by this episode that he decided to change his name. In the first half of the eighteenth century the word *roi* was not pronounced in the best circles as rhyming with *loi* but was pronounced "rouet." This assonance between his own name and that of the monarch irritated him, and he therefore invented for himself the anagram of "Voltaire" under which, after the successful performance of his tragedy *Oedipe,* he became immediately famous. His literary position was confirmed by the publication in 1723 of the *Henriade,* his epic of Henri IV. To our minds, both his plays and his epic are dreary reading, being composed of platitudes and wearisome versification, but to his contemporaries they seemed models of correct drama and poetry. They were unaware of the fact that Voltaire, as a writer, lacked both ear and passion and that his facile verses were both stilted and unmelodious. Already before he reached thirty he was acclaimed as a literary genius; the whole of Parisian so-

ciety lay at his feet.

It is not surprising that his early literary and social success should have turned the head of young Voltaire. He was always sensitive to flattery as he was hypersensitive to criticism. It may have been that he often allowed his conversational powers to run away with him and that his verbal and even his written epigrams caused offense. On one occasion, when supping with the Duc de Sully, he showed off vauntingly, and the Chevalier de Rohan, who resented his uppishness, exclaimed, "Who is that young man who talks so loud?" Voltaire replied that he was a man of letters and as such the equal even of the mighty family of Rohan. The Chevalier, incensed by this impertinence, ordered his footmen to seize Voltaire in the street and to give him a sound beating. The Chevalier watched this drubbing from his coach, peeping through silk curtains with a leer. Voltaire sent a challenge to the Chevalier, which was regarded as a further act of impertinence, since nobles, especially Rohans, did not fight duels with people so far below them in rank. A further *lettre de cachet* was obtained, and for the second time Voltaire was cast into the Bastille, for a period of six months. On his release he was ordered to leave Paris. He decided to visit England, then reputed to be the asylum of the persecuted and the island of the free. He landed at Greenwich in May, 1726, and remained in England until March, 1729.

On his return to France he wrote, although he did not yet dare to publish, his *Letters concerning the English,* in which

he had the audacity to suggest that the democratic institutions of England were preferable in practice and likely to last longer than the monolithic autocracy of France. When in 1734 a pirated edition of these Letters was issued in Paris, it was publicly burnt by order of the *parlement.* Voltaire was so alarmed by the outcry it provoked that he fled with Madame du Châtelet to her château at Cirey-sur-Blaise, which, being close to the Lorraine frontier, offered a convenient escape route should prosecution threaten.

Emilie de Breteuil had been forced by her family, when aged nineteen, to marry the Marquis du Châtelet, a professional soldier of amiable and accommodating disposition and small interest in intellectual pursuits. She herself was a mathematician and astonished French society by translating Newton's *Principia* and by writing several treatises on natural philosophy and sums. It was regarded as admirable but eccentric that a woman of such excellent family, who could have qualified for posts of the utmost distinction at Versailles, should have been content to exile herself to this bleak northeastern corner of France, to pay but slight attention to fashion or personal cleanliness, and be content to remain the avowed and faithful mistress of the commoner Voltaire for fourteen years. The manner of their domestic life at Cirey—the rigid timetable that they imposed upon themselves, the studies that occupied their days and nights—has been recorded by Madame de Graffigny, who stayed at Cirey for three months as an observant if unwelcome guest, and excellently described by Miss Nancy Mitford in a gay and scintillating book. When staying at the court of King Stanislas at Lunéville, they met the Comte de Saint-Lambert, a man who combined unusual charm and enterprise with a predilection for women who were past their first youth. It was he who had robbed Rousseau of Madame d'Houdetot and who now robbed Voltaire of Madame du Châtelet. The latter was well over forty and had lost her figure and her looks, having all her life devoted far more attention to the laws of gravity than to the preservation of her charms. One evening in October, 1748, Voltaire strolled casually into her sitting room and found her locked in the embraces of Saint-Lambert. After two or three hours of intense rage and mortification, the philosopher felt it wiser to accept the position. Madame du Châtelet was already pregnant, and in 1749 she died in childbirth. Voltaire was deeply afflicted by the loss of his old friend, but he was consoled by the friendly and tactful condolences of Saint-Lambert and by the fact that since 1745 he had been having an affair with his niece, Madame Denis.

Louise Mignot, the daughter of Voltaire's sister, had in 1738 married Monsieur Denis of the Commissariat Department, who died in 1744. Her uncle on the occasion of her marriage had presented her with a dowry of thirty thousand francs. On the death of Madame du Châtelet his niece became his mistress and constant companion; they lived together until the day of his death. His friends were perplexed by this infatuation. Madame Denis was ugly, unintelligent, a bad housekeeper, snobbish, and intellectually pretentious. It seemed strange indeed that Voltaire, who was so fastidious and tidy in his habits, could have loved, or even tolerated, this dull and slatternly woman. What was even worse, she had extravagant tastes, and Voltaire, who was careful about money, much resented her gift for ostentation and the lavish expenditure which she indulged in when hostess at Ferney. She had no taste for country life and was not reticent in expressing her longing for Paris. In fact in 1768 Voltaire gave her leave of absence for eighteen months, and profited by the interlude to cut down expenditure and to give to Ferney a thorough spring-cleaning. On her uncle's death she became his residuary legatee. She immediately disposed of Ferney and sold his library to Catherine the Great. Being now an heiress, she married a young man of the name of du Vivier: she died unlamented in 1790.

Voltaire himself was happy in the comparative seclusion of Ferney. Being only three and a half miles from Geneva, it offered an easy escape in the event of danger. He acquired the property in 1758 and lived there magnificently for the next twenty years. He built a private theater, became interested in agriculture and gardening, started a watch factory for the relief of unemployment, had an excellent cook, kept sixty servants, and entertained lavishly. He would sometimes argue that it was in order to please Madame Denis that he had turned himself into "the innkeeper of Europe." In fact he was delighted that his home should become a place of pilgrimage for international intellectuals. La Harpe came and stayed for a year; the great actress Mlle Clairon came, and d'Alembert, and Con-

dorcet, and Dr. Burney; Charles James Fox came and charmed Voltaire as he charmed everybody; Boswell came and fired such insistent questions at Voltaire that he pretended to have a fainting fit in order to rid himself of so bumptious an interviewer; the Emperor of Austria, Joseph II, actually drove past the gates of Ferney without calling. Voltaire regarded this as "a disgrace."

It was during the Madame du Châtelet period that Voltaire spent some uneasy months at the court of Versailles. In 1744 the Duc de Richelieu had suggested to him that it might be useful if he wrote a play to celebrate the marriage of the Dauphin with the Infanta of Spain. He therefore composed *La Princesse de Navarre,* and in order to adjust his verses to the music specially composed for the occasion by Rameau, and to supervise the production and the scenery, he was accorded a tiny little room in the palace, adjoining the latrines of the Swiss Guard. Madame du Châtelet, being by birth a Breteuil, was more comfortably housed. He took some pains to win the favor of Louis XV and Madame de Pompadour and even went so far as to write adulatory verses to the Pope. He was appointed Historiographer Royal, and a Gentleman of the Chamber. Having by these means rendered himself a respectable member of society, he was elected a member of the French Academy in 1746 when fifty-two years of age. He was unhappy at Versailles. He wrote to Madame Denis complaining that he was bored to death by court society and the conversation of the great. "I have," he wrote, "to deal with twenty actors, the opera, the ballet, the decorations. And for what purpose? To get a passing nod from the Dauphine." He ended by referring to Versailles as "the place that I abhor."

The climax was reached when they were all at Fontainebleau playing cards in one of the salons. Madame du Châtelet enjoyed gambling, but chess was the only game in which Voltaire indulged. Nor did he relish late hours and overheated rooms. Madame du Châtelet was seated at the card table of the Duc de Richelieu with other courtiers. Voltaire took a chair and sat behind her, hoping that the game would soon be over. When she had lost eighty thousand livres his patience snapped. "Why," he hissed at her, "must you persist in playing with a gang of cheats?" Realizing that his remark had been overheard and that the outraged courtiers would obtain a *lettre de cachet*

against him, entailing a third period of incarceration in the Bastille, he and Madame du Châtelet left the card table, hurried to their rooms where they gathered a few things together, and escaped that very night to Sceaux, where they were hidden by the Duchesse du Maine until the storm subsided. In vain did Voltaire strive to avert vengeance by writing adulatory verses to Madame de Pompadour. The Queen was incensed by this tribute to her rival, and the King, feeling that his private affairs were not fit subject for public poems, was also annoyed. On January 13, 1748, having recovered from his panic, Voltaire summoned up courage again to appear at Court. The courtiers turned their backs upon him and he realized that the disfavor into which he had fallen was bound to lead to punishment. He therefore drove with Madame du Châtelet to Cirey and eventually crossed the frontier into Lorraine and took refuge with King Stanislas at Lunéville. It was there that they encountered Saint-Lambert and that the final tragedy (or was it a liberation?) occurred.

The satire which Voltaire directed against the shams and follies of his age, contrasting with his almost subservient conformity in regard to the established order, has exposed him to the charge of insincerity. He was, it is true, capable of stratagems and evasions as tortuous as those of the Pope himself. His sallies and epigrams were often cruel, and he took pleasure in shocking the feelings of the ordinary man. *La Pucelle* has often been condemned as an outrageous lampoon, and we must agree that Joan of Arc is not a fit subject for salacious ridicule. He was a pugnacious and litigious man, and his quarrels with Jean Jacques Rousseau and Frederick the Great were attended by a degree of publicity which, it must regretfully be admitted, was not wholly unwelcome to him. We must remember that by his French contemporaries he was regarded as a mighty poet and as their greatest dramatist since Racine; to this day French critics deplore that so serious a writer should have descended to the trivial, the mean, or the jocose. Yet, however monkeylike may have been his gestures, jokes, and impulses, his deep and wide influence was founded on a passionate hatred of stupidity and injustice. His life-long motto, his signature tune, if one may use such an expression, was *Ecrasez l'infâme,* by which he meant a battle to the death with every form of intellectual, doctrinal, or social intolerance: "To Voltaire," writes John Morley, "an irrational prejudice was not the object of a polite coldness, but a real evil to be combated and overthrown at every hazard. Cruelty was not to him a disagreeable dream of the imagination . . . but a vivid flame burning into his thoughts and destroying peace. Wrongdoing and injustice were not simple words on his lips; they went as knives to the heart."

It was not personal oppression only that enraged him: all his life he fought against any form of obscurantism which "might extinguish a single ray from the great sun of knowledge." To him "reason and humanity were but a single word and love of truth and passion for justice but one emotion." Under his influence men of letters began to question all established institutions and conventions. He was pioneer and patron of a mighty intellectual rebellion. He marks an epoch in himself.

Consider, above all, the dangerous but unremitting battle that he waged on behalf of the victims of intolerance. In 1724 he had intervened to save the Abbé Desfontaines who had been accused of homosexuality, the penalty for which was to be burnt alive. The Abbé never forgave Voltaire for having rescued him from the fagots and in later years became one of his most vindictive enemies. But Voltaire was not deterred by such ingratitude. When Admiral Byng was sentenced to be shot on his own quarter-deck in order to assuage a burst of popular indignation, Voltaire persuaded his successful antagonist, the Duc de Richelieu, to write an open letter in the Admiral's defense. In 1762, in the fanatical city of Toulouse, the Huguenot Jean Calas was accused of having murdered his own son, although everybody knew that the boy was a manic depressive who had committed suicide. The whole family were cast into a dungeon and kept in irons for five months. The father, then sixty-three years old, was tortured and finally had all his limbs broken with iron bars. The younger daughters were interned in convents. The youngest son, Donat, then a lad of fifteen, managed to escape into Switzerland, where he appealed to Voltaire to clear his father's name. With tremendous vigor Voltaire started the great Calas campaign. He wrote letters to everybody; he published pamphlets; he started a public subscription extracting contributions from such diverse figures as the Empress of Russia, the King of Poland, and

It is not always easy to imagine Voltaire in the role of country squire, but that is how he lived for twenty years at Ferney—and was depicted by the Swiss painter Huber.

even George III of England. He enlisted the sympathy of Madame de Pompadour, the Duc de Richelieu, and the Duc de Choiseul. After conducting his campaign for three years (during which, as he asserted, he never allowed himself to smile) the innocence of the late Calas was vindicated by the Council of Paris, and M. David de Beaudrigue, who as chief magistrate of Toulouse had been responsible for this atrocity, was dismissed from his post and committed suicide. Calas's two daughters were restored to their mother, and the fame of Voltaire as the champion of justice was blazoned throughout Europe.

In 1766 he denounced an even more flagrant case of intolerance, when the young Chevalier de La Barre was accused at Abbeville of irreverence in failing to uncover and kneel at the passage of a religious procession. He was tortured, his tongue was torn out, his head cut off, and his body committed to the flames. With him was burnt the *Philosophical Dictionary* of Voltaire, which they said had been the cause of his irreverence. Voltaire was both enraged and alarmed by this incident and for a few weeks escaped into Switzerland and took refuge at Rolle in the canton of Vaud. From there he wrote and published one of the most blistering of all his pamphlets, denouncing the execution of La Barre under the title "The Cry of Innocent Blood."

His final battle was on behalf of Lally-Tollendal, who begged him to clear the memory of his father, General Lally, who

had been defeated by Clive in India, had been accused on his return to Paris of having sold Pondicherry to the English, had been thrown into the Bastille and thereafter beheaded on the Place de Grève. Here again, by agitation and pamphlets, Voltaire succeeded in obtaining posthumous justice. On May 26, 1778, Louis XV pronounced that Lally had been unjustly condemned. That was the last of Voltaire's victories. He was already on his deathbed when Lally-Tollendal came to tell him that the reputation of his father had been cleared. Voltaire was satisfied that in his own century he had witnessed the triumph of the Age of Reason. "It is certain," he wrote, "that the knowledge of nature, the sceptical attitude towards old fables dignified by the name of history, a healthy metaphysic freed from the absurdities of the schools, are the fruits of that century when reason was perfected."

It is as the champion of the oppressed that I like to think of Voltaire, rather than as the sneering philosopher of the Houdon statue, or as the mischievous monkey of Potsdam. I like to think of the cheering crowds who on July 10, 1791, watched his coffin being drawn to the Panthéon, and I share the enthusiasm of those who cheered the inscription on his catafalque: "He taught us to be free."

Harold Nicolson's many books have included biographies, novels, and personal memoirs. His study of Voltaire will appear later this spring in The Age of Reason *(Doubleday).*

By OLIVER JENSEN

YOUR FRIENDLY FIDVCIARY

There isn't much to hang onto these days. Take banks. It seems only yesterday, in a sense, that the greatest banker of all, J. P. Morgan, left us for the Last Directors' Meeting. Indeed, no one has had the heart to break the news to the Soviet cartoonists, so that the old image—silk hat, wing collar, diamond stickpin, and bags of gold—lives on in many places.

Everyone knew, so very recently, how to tell a bank. It looked like a Roman temple, at least from the front. There were columns, polished brass, and at the fancier fiduciaries, female statuary robed loosely in the style of A.D. 300. All the ladies in this kind of nineteenth-century Greco-Roman art form have the same face. They served colleges as Muses, law courts as Justice, and in banks, I always supposed, they represented Fiscal Stability, or Compound Interest, or maybe The Resumption of Specie Payments. But this was only the beginning of the imperial note, which was rendered absolutely unmistakable by the lettering on the pediment, cut into stone in big Latin capitals with scrupulous attention to the rule that the Romans wrote V when they meant U. The fact that they didn't have a W or J, or use K much either, was quietly ignored to avoid making things difficult in places like Vashington, D.C., and Iacsonville, Fla. New York, or

Iorc, however, abounded with MANVFACTVRERS TRVST branches, and lord knows how many GVARANTY's; the latter is a lot easier to pronounce if you are a small boy trying to get things right: *Guh-varanty*. It sounded imposing, like *Suh-vub* Treasury, or Bank of the Vee-nited States; but in mouthing the latter, doubt began to enter even the most literal mind. A good thing, perhaps, since that imposing-sounding depository turned out, during the Depression, to be as bare as Old Mother Hvbbard's Cvpboard.

Old-time banks went in heavily for marble, high ceilings, and a deep cathedral hush. Customers spoke in low tones in order not to disturb the money, and the religious air was heightened by the guard who stood like a verger at the door of the steel vault. Behind all those bolts and wheels and dials lay the holy of holies, full of the bigger bills, the senior securities, and the choicest mortgages. Off to one side, in an atmosphere of plush and mahogany, sat The Officials, and one could detect the higher ranks by the white piping on the vests. You saw them again on Sunday morning, forsaking Caesar's collections for the moment and passing the plate, in spats. Formality was the keynote.

Well, you know what's happened. Now everything is glass, abstract art, and bonhomie. Come in and make friends at the

NICHOLAS SOLOVIOFF

Chase Manhattan. Drop in at our comfy Mortgage & Loan Department. Meet the fellows. See our fashion show, our ice ballet. Let us introduce you to the money.

It all started, I suspect, just the way the deep-dyed conservatives always expected, with Government Interference. One minute the New Deal was guaranteeing deposits, and the next thing anyone knew, there was a mural painter at work in the lobby. Then the Government took away the right of private banks to issue their own paper money, and the senior vice-presidents who used to sign the bills had nothing to do any more. They began to buy art, like David Rockefeller of the Chase, and this, of course, got them to meeting modern architects, and that was the end of the Roman temples. With the glass walls it has become possible to see any banker in New York, indeed, impossible not to see him. The lower echelons of officials are ranged right alongside the wall in such a way that any passerby can read the papers on their desks, and it is difficult to maintain the old air of secrecy, let alone hitch up one's socks or take a little unobserved nap. The money itself has no privacy at all.

Given all this sudden and violent change in tradition, it was obvious that bankers would get to know one another and start merging. The process has gone so far that it is almost as hard to recognize the banks by their names as it is by their buildings. If American bankers, like English ones, used their own names—Messrs. Coutts, Barclay's, Williams Deacon's, and the like—merging would offer no problems of nomenclature, but here it has been necessary to make up all sorts of unlikely combinations. The best example is the union of the Chemical Bank & Trust Company with the Corn Exchange Bank, producing "Chemical Corn." The old image, in both cases, was dignified—thoughtful professors, metallurgists, and inventors dropping into the Chemical Bank to make a deposit, perhaps even to suggest some new advance in alchemy, which the bank, one imagines, followed up with special zeal. Up at the Corn Exchange, on the other hand, fantasy pictures sturdy farmers pulling up the horses and dropping in to salt away the proceeds of the fall crop and conceivably exchange a few bushels of the Favored Commodity for, say, the bank's calendar and a winter's supply of deposit slips. But the new image! Chemical Corn! As if

every child did not know this cheap confection, sold ten kernels for the penny and not a very convincing imitation at that.

The heartiness of modern banking is overwhelming, if advertising means anything. You never know whether you are going in to make a small withdrawal or to take part in a wienie roast. Every night on television the First National City Bank of New York reminds one and all that at their far-flung institutions, "You come first!" It is an interesting, Orwellian idea—everyone first, but some, perhaps, more first than others?—although it suggests certain problems of implementation on days when there are long lines at the tellers' windows. There lurks in this slogan, somehow, an implied, mysterious comparison. What comes first at other banks, eh? Does it mean to plant the suspicion that the money-changers in other temples are a mite less friendly, a little less full of the first-name, shirt-sleeve spirit? Who comes second, by the way, at First National City?

But it is petty to question the jargon of modern institutional *Gemütlichkeit*, which has been designed for imprecision ever since the first "better" was used without its "than." The bank is just trying to tell you that it's big and friendly, like a dog, and wants to nuzzle up. And any day now the Christmas Club will hold a taffy-pull, and maybe get up a blazer.

The best way to visualize the change that has taken place, apparently overnight, is to try to re-create J. P. Morgan in the new image. He is sitting behind a little modernistic table—it seems a little dainty for a desk, but that's what it is—and the substantial bottom is perched (is there a trace of unease in the furrowed countenance?) on a fragile contraption of wire and laminated bamboo shoots, designed for him by a clever Japanese. He has on a tweed jacket, suede shoes, and button-down shirt, and he leaps up to greet you, the new depositor. "We're all plain folks here," he booms. "Make yourself comfortable while I get you some coffee and a plastic piggy bank for the kiddies."

Then the face that launched a thousand mergers turns toward you. Beneath the bushy brows and steely eyes there suddenly spreads the smile of Your Friendly Naborhood Banker. "By the way," Morgan says, "just call me Jack."

FRASCONI'S BRIO WITH A BOOK

For an artist who habitually pictures himself as a melancholy fellow contemplating the passing scene somewhat quizzically (as in the self-portrait at far left), Antonio Frasconi has created a joyous woodcut world populated by drolly fearsome beasts, gaily plumaged birds, and poet-heroes, all warmed by benevolently anthropomorphic suns. A selection of his work appears on this and the following pages.

Since his arrival in the United States from Uruguay in 1945 at the age of twenty-six, Frasconi has exercised a pervasive influence upon print making, leading the way in a revitalization of the medieval art of the woodcut. Today he is perhaps its foremost American master, his individual prints sought by private collectors and exhibited in the principal museums of the country. Less known to the public, but no less esteemed by connoisseurs, are Frasconi's woodcut books.

Frasconi has cherished books and printing since his boy-

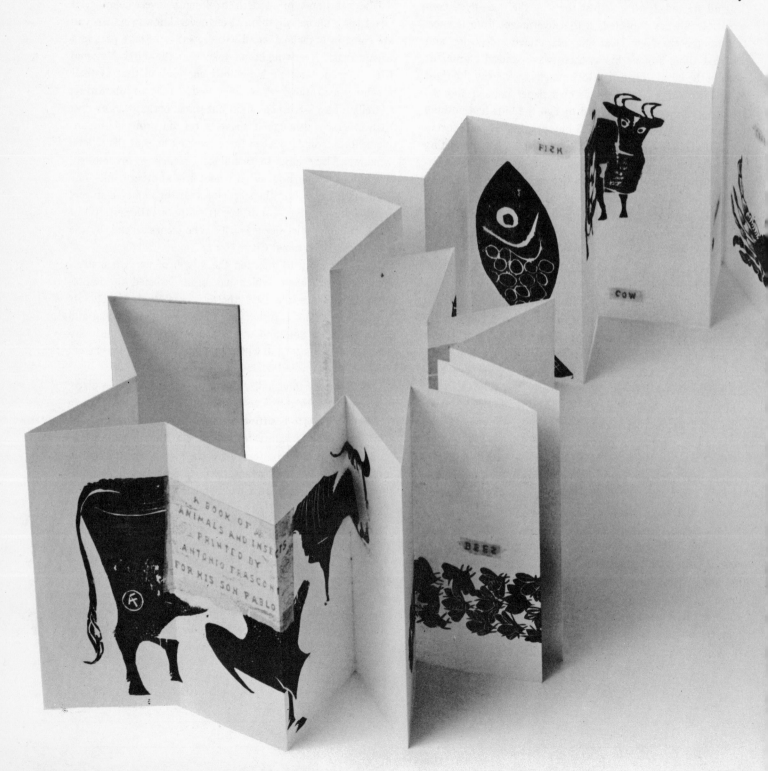

hood in Montevideo, where his Italian parents had settled, and where he took his first job, at twelve, as a printer's apprentice. A richly self-educated man, he has sought to pass on his feeling for books to his two young sons, the eldest of whom (nine-year-old Pablo, named after the artist's idol, Picasso) is portrayed at left by his father. For Pablo, Frasconi has made by hand a series of unique books—there is but one copy of each—picturing for the boy the natural world the artist observes so scrupulously and renders so freshly. Often printed on Japanese folding paper, they range from the bestiary shown in the photograph below—its labels were directly impressed from alphabet-soup letters—to the book of wood-block acrobats and the volume printed from biscuits, etc., both of which are illustrated overleaf.

Because he exhibits at the gallery of the eminent New York bookman E. Weyhe, Frasconi's work quickly came to the attention of bibliophiles, and several exquisite books of limited edition have now been printed from his original blocks. These include *Birds from My Homeland*, 1958, one of whose prints is reproduced on pages 126–127, and, last year, *A Whitman Portrait*: one of its fourteen different woodcuts of the poet appears on page 125. The latter is the second in a series which Frasconi is devoting to major figures in American letters—the first was *The Face of Edgar Allan Poe*, 1959. But despite the attractions of having his art published widely, Frasconi persists in making and printing books of either one copy or, very rarely, several, at his studio in Norwalk, Connecticut. As various as his *Homage to Thelonius Monk*, the jazz musician, and *A Book of Many Suns* (one of the suns is illustrated on page 128), each exults in Frasconi's creed: "to communicate in my work what is dearest to me; not death but life itself and the greatness of being alive."

Antonio Frasconi has a craftsman's respect for his materials and is a traditionalist in his desire to see his woodcut prints preserve the rough character of the wood and the strokes of the knife (as in the portrait of Whitman at right, and in a fold-out book of acrobats done for his son Pablo, a portion of which is shown above). But occasionally he diverts himself with new media. As another entertainment for his children, Frasconi put together an entire book which he titled *Printing with Dough*. Each page is a design taken from such baked goods as animal crackers or Hydrox cookies (below) which were inked, covered with a sheet of colored paper, and printed by rubbing a spoon over the back of the paper.

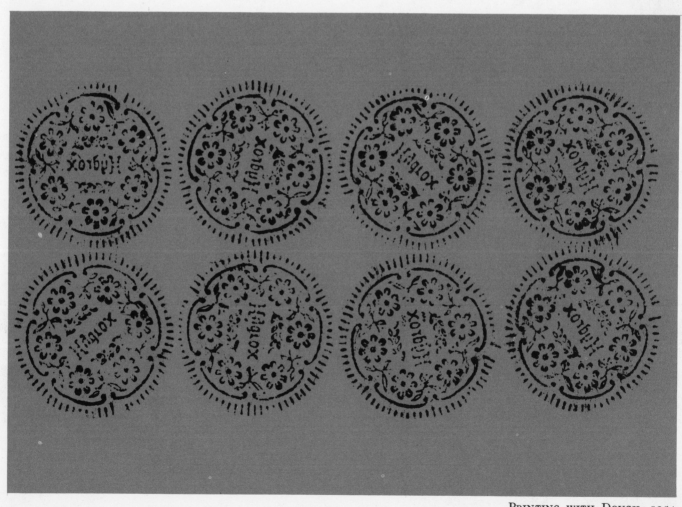

PRINTING WITH DOUGH, 1954

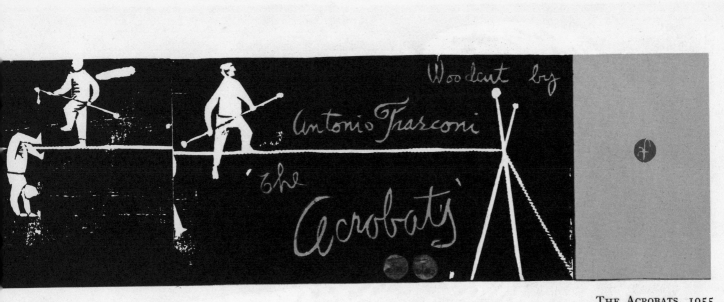

THE ACROBATS, 1955

A WHITMAN PORTRAIT, 1960

Calandria

BIRDS FROM MY HOMELAND, 1958

A Book of Many Suns, 1953